Managerial Judgement and Strategic Investment Decisions

Managerial Judgement and Strategic Investment Decisions

A Cross-Sectional Survey

Elaine P. Harris
Clive R. Emmanuel
and
Samuel Komakech

ELSEVIER

AMSTERDAM • BOSTON • HEIDELBERG • LONDON • NEW YORK • OXFORD
PARIS • SAN DIEGO • SAN FRANCISCO • SINGAPORE • SYDNEY • TOKYO
CIMA Publishing is an imprint of Elsevier

CIMA PUBLISHING

CIMA Publishing is an imprint of Elsevier
Linacre House, Jordan Hill, Oxford OX2 8DP, UK
30 Corporate Drive, Suite 400, Burlington, MA 01803, USA

First edition 2009

British Library Cataloguing in Publication Data
A catalogue record for this book is available from the British Library

Library of Congress Cataloging-in-Publication Data
A catalog record for this book is available from the Library of Congress

ISBN: 978-1-85617-823-5

For information on all CIMA publications visit our website at elsevierdirect.com

Transferred to digital printing in 2009.

Contents

About the Authors

Prof. Elaine P. Harris is Professor and Head of Department of Accounting and Finance and Head of Leicester Business School's Graduate Centre at De Montfort University. She was Chair of the Committee of Heads of Accounting (CHA) (2005–2009), past secretary of the Management Control Association (MCA) and a member of CIMA's Lifelong Learning Policy Committee. Her research interests are in project risk assessment and decision-making. She is guest editor of the *International Journal of Risk Assessment and Management* and managing editor (special issues) of *The Journal of Applied Accounting Research.*

Prof. Clive R. Emmanuel is Professor of Accounting and Finance at the University of Glasgow. He is currently joint editor of the *British Accounting Review*. His research interests are in management control, transfer pricing and capital budgeting. He has published extensively in the UK and international journals.

Samuel Komakech is Lecturer in Accounting and Finance at De Montfort University and worked as the research assistant on this CIMA-funded project, while studying for his PhD. He has worked in Uganda as a tax consultant for KPMG and teaches management accounting. His research interests are in activity-based costing and capital budgeting.

About the Authors

Acknowledgements

The authors gratefully acknowledge the research funding provided by CIMA General Charitable Trust that enabled this study to be undertaken, and participation of CIMA members in the survey. We are also very grateful to the anonymous reviewers whose helpful comments enabled us to improve the earlier version of this report.

List of Figures and Tables

Figures

Tables

Executive Summary

Introduction

This book presents the findings of a cross-sectional survey on strategic investment decision (SID) making funded by CIMA. The book contains a review of literature on the SID process and on the aspects of managerial judgement that may be brought to bear by the managers involved in that process. It describes the survey design and discusses the analysis of responses and implications of key findings. It includes suggestions for improving the SID process and the practice of management in relation to different types of project.

Strategic investment decisions

In this research, we define SIDs as decisions concerning long-term investment in assets, e.g. purchase of new buildings, technology or equipment, business ventures or knowledge acquisition in pursuance of the organisation's strategic objectives. They are arguably the most important decisions organisations make, characterised by novelty, complexity, irreversibility and potentially, the huge sums of money invested. As each strategic option or project opportunity is likely to be different, they are also distinguished from other more routine decisions, such as pricing or promotion, by high levels of uncertainty. In attempts to overcome this uncertainty, managers naturally rely on their past experience of similar events, their professional expertise and the judgement of others (who may be consulted in the process) as well as their own. Thus the SID process can take up considerable management time over an extended period before a decision is finally reached.

There may be 10 or more stages in the SID process, from scanning for project opportunities to post-implementation review, with formal evaluation using discounted cash flow techniques only possible more than halfway through, after the proposition has been defined and researched and sufficient data has been collected to make the necessary assumptions. Much early discussion by managers therefore takes place before this evidence is available, such that early judgements may be intuitive, based on past experience and industry norms. These early judgements may or may not change as more and better evidence surfaces later in the process.

SIDs can be categorised as falling into a broad typology of project types, which managers may have previous experience of. Common types of SID include:

- New product development
- New market development (new customers/clients)
- New site or site development (operating facilities, e.g. new location, relocation and expansion)
- New technology or infrastructure (e.g. computer system development/replacement)
- Acquisition of business assets or companies
- Compliance (new legislation, e.g. health and safety)

The SID process has been explored in its organisational context through case studies, which has revealed some of the behaviours underlying managerial judgement, though often by accident rather than by design. The concepts of heuristics, framing bias and consensus have been developed by psychologists with an interest in explaining decision-making behaviour, but have not featured strongly in management accounting studies, especially in surveys.

Managerial judgement

Heuristics are defined as a set of simplifying assumptions by which managers can draw on their knowledge and experience to form intuitive judgements under conditions of uncertainty. We asked questions about the use of industry rules of thumb, use of base values and tolerance ranges (known in psychology as anchoring and adjustment), and the balance of intuition vs. evaluation in assessing the risk profile of a prospective project.

Framing refers to the way that information about a prospective project is presented and how managers bring their preferences to bear in the processing of that information, displaying bias towards initial information (primacy), more recent information (recency) or sticking to the status quo. Individuals may also react differently to the framing of a prospect depending on their risk appetite, and how positively or negatively the risk is expressed. We asked questions about sources of information and what influenced managers' views.

Consensus may be reached by managers sharing information and views in different ways, through formal and informal meetings, and through political lobbying by project champions canvassing for support. Different stakeholder groups may present their views whether formally consulted or not. We asked questions about group processes and important factors in reaching agreement in the respondents' experience.

Key findings

The survey resulted in 91 usable responses spread across 65 companies in 24 industries. The company response rate of 16%, though less than ideal, gives us a sufficient sample from which to gain useful insights about SID practice in a reasonable number of UK companies.

A content analysis of the job titles revealed a total of 55 accounting and finance specialists, including 21 finance directors. There were 6 CEOs, 1 chairman, 3 MDs, 8 other directors and 4 vice presidents amongst the 22 senior general management roles. Whilst all respondents were in fairly senior roles, over half were in more senior roles.

The most common types of project experienced by respondents, which also formed their focus for answering the behavioural questions, were:

1. New technology or infrastructure projects
2. New site or site development
3. Business acquisitions
4. New product development
5. New market development

The vast majority of sample companies have formal SID-making processes. There was strong evidence to support the 10-stage model of the SID process presented in the questionnaire.

Senior managers are more likely to be involved in stages 4 and 9, shaping the project outline and authorising the project, and less senior managers are more likely to be involved in stages 3, 7 and 8, the data generation, analysis and persuasion points in the process.

Ninety-eight per cent report having formal meetings within the company to discuss SIDs. Other (non-financial) managers involved in these formal meetings were business development managers (49%), finance managers (81%), marketing managers (29%), IT managers (40%), operations managers (59%), project managers (61%) and production managers (28%).

A possibly surprising feature is the involvement of external parties in these formal meetings. A majority (64%) indicated their organisations hold meetings with consultants (39%), suppliers (30%), customers (16%), financiers (16%) and government departments (15%). Sixty-four per cent of respondents are personally involved in such meetings with these other organisations where the outside managers are project managers (23%), finance managers (21%), business development managers (19%) and operations managers (19%) in these other organisations.

The most frequent purpose of these formal meetings appears to be to:

- Evaluate the risk of the project
- Reach a decision on the desirability of the project
- Identify key success factors
- Gather views from constituencies and stakeholders

In terms of project types, external accountants and lawyers are more likely to be consulted in business acquisitions, and suppliers in the case of new technology investments.

There was a high level of support for the presence of certain psychological attributes, with 69% using brainstorming techniques and 67% using mental pictures of the SID. Less significant, but still notable is the 52% who report drawing on intuition (gut feelings, hunches or flashes of ideas). Eighty-one per cent make comparisons with previous experience, and 66% use these as base values or tolerances ranges, which exemplify anchoring and adjustment.

Notable sources of information accessed for specific projects are information on customers (86%), financial projections and business risk factors (both 95%), and supply chain information (78%), but less information was available on shareholders' views (32%). Seventy-nine per cent found the pace of decision-making problematic and 69% were influenced by updated financial projections, the recency of which changed their views on the project.

There is interesting evidence of political behaviour within organisations. For example, 57% witness temporary alliances forming to a significant extent and 69% report 'corridor' meetings or the equivalent as well as the views of superior managers being influential (82%). The use of mental pictures is most common in new product or new market development projects, and brainstorming is more common in new product development and new technology projects.

In apparent contrast, there is a high level of use of formal systems, including decision support software. Factors which respondents thought were important in gaining consensus were:

- managers who speak their minds forthrightly (88%)
- managers with very different skills (78%)
- like-minded managers with similar experience in the industry (78%)
- managers with very different experiences (74%)
- managers trained in negotiating skills (64%)

Conclusions

- There is widespread support for an emerging model of the SID process, involving accountants and other managers in up to 10 stages, of which the application of project appraisal techniques is just one.
- There are two additional stages, not previously recognised in the SID literature, an implementation and testing phase before the post-implementation review stage, and a change management phase to sustain and embed the benefits of the project, especially in business acquisitions.
- Companies tend to require standard SID procedures, with assumptions stated explicitly in order to obtain top management approval, but few require dissenting opinions to be reported.
- Most companies (90%) now use spreadsheet models to support SID-making, and half use critical path analysis (project management software). Whilst few use specialist decision aid software, only 6% use no decision support software at all.
- 37 respondents (41%) made some suggestions for improvement to the SID process in their company, one stated that no improvements were necessary, and the remainder chose not to reply to this free text question. The most common calls are for greater compliance, better timing or wider consultation.
- There is an increasing need for managers to consult various parties external to the organisation on whom the success of the project may rely, especially in acquisitions where the quality of external information, e.g. financial and legal, is critical, or new site/technology projects where suppliers are consulted.
- There is almost as much evidence of psychological and socio-political processes (heuristics, framing and consensus) involved in strategic decisions as there is for the formal financial projections and project appraisal techniques. Strategic decisions were found to involve cognitive processes as well as formal analytical models.
- There is significant use of brainstorming (especially in new product development or technology projects) and mental pictures (heuristics), especially in new product/market development type projects.
- Influence from market research, customer and supply chain information (framing) is significant, and importance is attached to the views of top company management and managers who speak their minds forthrightly. In contrast, there is similar importance attached to like-minded managers with similar industry experience as there is to managers with very different skills. There is little evidence of status quo bias among our respondents, as half reported changing their views as a result of receiving more up-to-date information, and over 80% reported factors altering their opinions.
- Business risk factors are as important in the framing of projects as the financial projections (both had 95% support). Prior to Collier et al. (2007) studies either found little evidence of formal risk analysis or ignored the issue.

Introduction

This book presents the findings from a cross-sectional survey funded by CIMA. The project aimed to survey senior management accountants working across a range of organisations and industries with a unique focus on the behavioural side of decision-making, the use of managerial judgement. Previous capital budgeting surveys have tended to focus on the quantitative evaluation tools and techniques used for project appraisal. This study was broader in that it asked about every stage of the strategic investment decision (SID) process, from initiation to post-implementation review, and how different managers were involved at different stages of the process. The focus is on how decision judgements are reached.

Chapter 1 introduces the subject of SIDs by providing a review of relevant literature. It defines different types of SID and sets the SID process in the organisational context in which decision-making takes place. It examines the role of multiple managers in the process and the stages that a typical SID might go through.

Chapter 2 identifies and describes the key psychological concepts that determine managerial behaviour as it impacts upon the SID process. It examines the use of heuristics and possible sources of bias, and raises questions about how SIDs are presented or framed. It also positions SID-making as a collective socio-political process, where many managers and external parties may influence the outcome of project appraisal. It sets the scene for the behavioural focus of this study, which asks about how consensus is reached in SIDs.

Chapter 3 describes the survey design and explains how the questions were derived from the literature outlined in Chapters 1 and 2. It provides information on the sample and the respondents and techniques used to analyse the data. The full questionnaire is provided in Appendix 1.

Chapter 4 presents the survey analysis, organised in five main sections. Firstly the types of SID, the stages in and nature of the SID process are reported. Then the managers' involvement is analysed, followed by the psychological and group processes. Findings are summarised and discussed, with the aggregate responses provided in Appendix 2 and the further statistical analysis in Appendix 3.

Chapter 5 summarises the key findings from the survey and suggests the implications for academics, accountants, managers and stakeholders in organisations. The suggestions made by respondents for improving the SID process in their organisations are highlighted.

The number and nature of these suggestions demonstrate the potential for improvement in practice in terms of how SIDs are made. Finally, a descriptive model of the SID process is presented. The application of this model is illustrated through the analysis of six case studies in Appendix 4 which shows how useful the model might be in guiding future research on SIDs.

Chapter 1

Strategic Investment Decisions

Introduction

This chapter contains a summary of the literature on strategic investment decisions (SIDs), also referred to as capital budgeting and investment appraisal. It includes definitions of key terms, a short historical review of the research undertaken in this important area of management accounting and the issues that have been observed in the practical application of models and techniques in organisations. It is focused on the organisational context in which SIDs take place, the process of SID-making and the involvement of managers in the process.

Context

Organisations need to invest continuously if they are to create value and to survive. Investment is thus a lifeline for organisations; however, it is a lifeline only if an organisation chooses the right projects. In this research we define SIDs as decisions concerning long-term investment in assets, e.g. purchase of new buildings, technology or equipment, business ventures or knowledge acquisition in pursuance of the organisation's strategic objectives. Consequently SIDs are the most important decisions that managers have to make, and poor quality decisions may prove disastrous and lead to the collapse of their organisations. The various types of SIDs are explained later in this chapter.

The organisational context for SIDs will vary in terms of the size, industry, aims, structure and culture of the organisation. SIDs can take place in small- and medium-sized businesses as well as large multinational corporations, not for profit, public services or government-owned organisations. However, there are common characteristics in terms of the process and techniques used for evaluating investment opportunities, and in all but the smallest micro-firm there will be more than one manager involved in the SID process. This means that the 'principal-agency problem' (managers acting on behalf of the owners of the enterprise) is a common issue. Managers are deciding to commit funds invested by the company shareholders or other investors, not their own money. This leads to a variety of behavioural issues, previously barely acknowledged by writers in management accounting.

The most common characteristic of SIDs, whatever the organisational context, is the need to evaluate the future impact of decisions in an uncertain environment. A variety of techniques may be used to analyse the costs and income or other benefits to be derived from the investment. Much past research has focused upon ascertaining which of these techniques, such as accounting rate of return, net present value (NPV) or internal rate of return (IRR) are used by management accountants in organisations. The problem of forecasting future cash flows and non-financial outcomes resulting from the decision means that SID-making is not an exact science, but an exercise in estimation, open to error and to misjudgement. In attempts to overcome this uncertainty, managers naturally rely on their past experience of similar events, their professional expertise and the judgement of others (who may be consulted in the process) as well as their own.

Research in SIDs, often referred to as capital budgeting in the past, has evolved through a number of phases. Haka (2007) summarises these phases, from the early work on discounted cash flow (DCF) techniques in the 1950s, through operations research, to agency-based research in the 1980s, organisational research in the 1990s to inter-firm research in the 2000s.

The main issues Haka (2007, pp. 698–699) identifies in the historical development of capital budgeting are:

- Accounting vs. economic returns
- Agency issues
- Uncertainty

It can be seen from her subsequent analysis of research that much of the literature is centred upon the first of these with the recognition of present value techniques and the diffusion of discounting procedures. This work was almost entirely conducted from an economics perspective. There were over 35 survey-based studies designed to establish which techniques were used by organisations over a 40-year period.

Later organisational research examined capital budgeting processes, policies and practices, admitting the agency problem to SID research. The most significant finding from this modelling-based research was the information asymmetry problem, whereby managers hold and use private sources of information, not available to others in the organisation or to its owners. The behavioural implications of this problem may be compounded by reward systems that produce 'sub-optimal decision-making'. Experimental research has drawn upon the psychology of individual decision-making, especially the phenomenon of 'escalating commitment' (e.g. Staw, 1981) though very little work has been done on group level responses to the uncertainty problem and collective managerial judgement.

Stages in the SID process

Management accounting literature has tended to focus upon the investment evaluation stage of strategic decision-making, suggesting that DCF analysis is most important in guiding managers to the best decision. This tends to ignore much of the organisational context which is of equal importance. This research adopts an alternative perspective on what comprises an effective SID by focusing on the role of managerial judgement within the organisational context. King (1975), Haynes and Solomon (1962), Bower (1986) and more recently, Harris (1999) have argued that evaluation is but one stage within the SID process. Project generation, estimation of cash flows, progress through the organisation, authorisation and post-audit examination are, in many enterprises, formal or informal stages in the SID process.

King (1975) suggested that researchers in the field of finance take too narrow a view of capital budgeting, and continue to assume that decisions will be made based entirely on economic evaluation. This is logical where shareholder wealth maximisation is assumed to be the primary objective of the firm. However, within this economic paradigm, organisational behavioural issues are largely ignored as irrelevant to finance theory. King (1975) offered a view which placed investment appraisal within a strategic decision-making process. The process he depicted was based on his analysis of a case involving the addition of extra capacity in the chemicals division of a diversified group. He described the process as a sequence of six stages, from triggering, through screening and definition to evaluation, transmission and decision. The diagrammatic representation of the process does not, however, appear to have possible feedback loops. Nonetheless, King's process model represents one of the first attempts to recognise investment appraisal in the organisational context of the enterprise.

Pike and Neale (1996), on the other hand, depict a simple capital budgeting system as a five-stage process, from determination of the budget, through search and development to evaluation, authorisation and monitoring and control. This model has possible feedback loops. It allows a return from the evaluation stage to the search and development stage as one of four feedback loops, and allows for the possibility of an idea being generated out of the normal sequence, at stage 2, which causes management to consider an increase in the budget by looping back to stage 1. The model does not stop at the decision point, but adds a monitoring and control stage (post-audit), which loops back to the evaluation stage. This appears to be an improvement on earlier presentations of the process. However, in today's business environment, with the high level of capital needed to invest in advanced manufacturing technology (Eisenhardt, 1989), the concept of setting and adhering to an annual capital budget is perhaps outmoded, or at least restricted to projects which would not fit the definition of an SID.

An alternative view is offered in the strategic planning literature. Dyson (1990, p. 7) sets out 11 elements in the strategic decision-making process, which also includes feedback loops. Dyson focuses on six of these, from objective setting and review, strategic option formulation, and assessment of uncertainty, through corporate system model, performance measurement, to gap analysis and selection. He provides a matrix which positions 14 analytical techniques in terms of their potential impact at each stage. Capital investment appraisal is technique number 11, shown as having primary impact at the later stages in the process.

This approach separates out the financial analysis (performance measurement) from the decision analysis (gap analysis and selection), which overcomes Jones and Dugdale's (1994) criticism of accountants confusing measures and criteria. It also positions the techniques which are assumed to be in the accountants' domain as a minority of the 14 techniques that may be applied in strategic decision analysis. This raises a key question on the role of management accountants and the need to discover which stages they are involved in.

Harris (1999, p. 352) conducted empirical work on the strategic investment appraisal process and developed a model (Figure 1.1) which shows that very little of the process takes place at group level (stage 6), but is located within the divisional domain. *Executive judgement* is exercised at divisional level at two stages (3 and 5), an 'early screening' stage, once there is sufficient information to make a judgement as to whether the project is worth investigating fully, and the more formal stage when the decision is made to place the project on the group board agenda.

The authors have reviewed case-based research on SIDs undertaken over a 20-year period, analysing over 1,000 pages of evidence from 16 published studies covering over 300 SIDs for a further study. Of these, 11 studies gave a practice-based view of the SID process in multiple stages. The number of stages varied from three main phases (Bower, 1986) of initiation, integration and corporate, with sub-processes, to six main steps (Mintzberg et al., 1976) with an average of 9.7. The most recent (Harris, 1999) reported seven steps in an iterative process, including a post-audit stage, not included in most of the others. Haka (2007, p. 721) reviewed more than 12 studies on post-audit-related research, though few were case-based.

Box 1.1 shows the 10 stages in the SID process adopted for the purpose of this study. It is largely based on the seven steps in Harris (1999), with her 'ideas and opportunities' stage expanded into the first three, and her 'analysis and evaluation' stage expanded into the sixth and seventh stages.

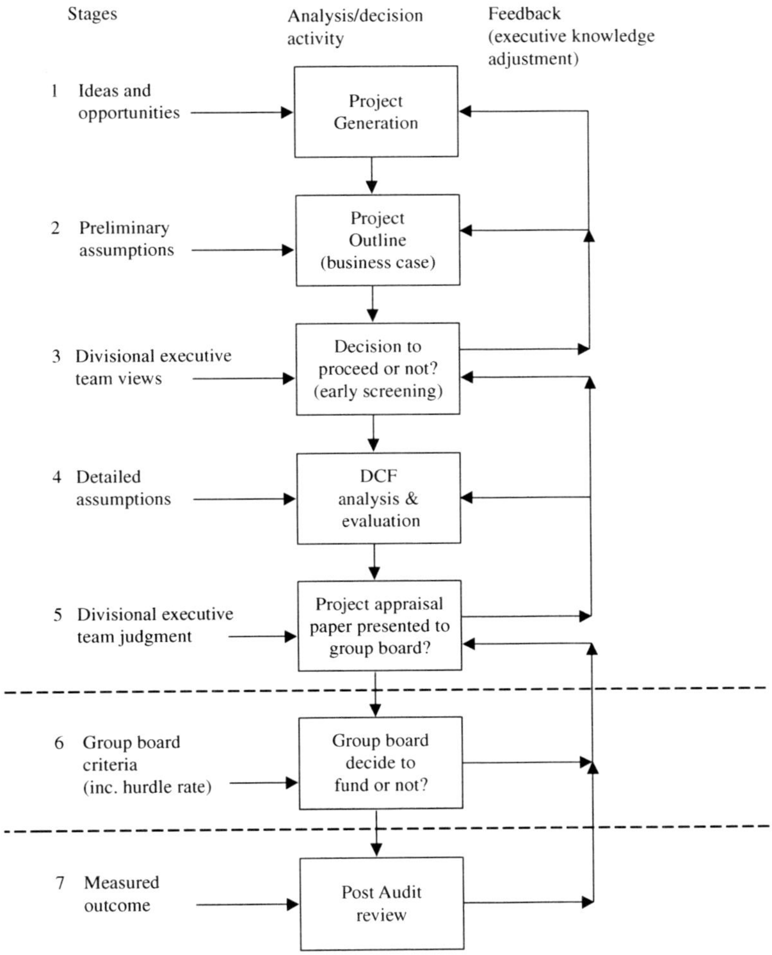

Figure 1.1 Strategic investment appraisal process
Source: Harris (1999)

BOX 1.1 STAGES IN THE SID PROCESS

1. Scanning for project opportunities
2. Defining possible projects and formulating strategic options
3. Generating project data
4. Making preliminary assumptions and shaping the project outline
5. Early screening to decide if project idea to be pursued
6. Estimation of cash flow/financial data based on detailed assumptions
7. Formal evaluation using DCF-based techniques
8. Progression through the company, persuading senior managers to support the project and submit it to the group board
9. Authorisation of the board (decision to support and fund the project)
10. Post-audit evaluation (project review)

Types of SID

Haka (2007, p. 698) defined investment appraisal as a process of evaluation of new investments "by which firms create value for their owners". Examples given of these types of long-term investments were:

- Machines
- Buildings
- Advertising campaigns
- Options to lease or buy
- Acquisitions
- Employee training
- Alliances and joint ventures

Whilst not all of these examples might be considered 'strategic' on their own (advertising or training for example), especially if the investment is of relatively small magnitude, the point is well made that "in combination these investments shape the firm's strategic direction". In most firms today, it can be argued that there is an identifiable strategy, whether documented and well communicated throughout the organisation or implicit in the actions and intentions displayed. From this and other past SID research, we compiled a list of seven types of SID, as shown in Box 1.2.

Multiple manager participation in the process

Placed in an organisational context, the SID has the potential to involve many managers with differing degrees of seniority, functional experience and industry-specific knowledge. Half of the case-based studies we reviewed reported the involvement

BOX 1.2 TYPES OF SID

- New product development
- New market development (new customers/clients)
- New site or site development (operating facilities, e.g. new location, relocation and expansion)
- New technology or infrastructure (e.g. computer system development/replacement)
- Acquisition of business assets or companies
- Compliance (new legislation, e.g. health and safety)
- Others (e.g. decommissioning, downsizing and business process redesign)

of multiple managers in the SID process, and 75% of cases made observations on SID-making as a social or political process involving a need for managers to reach agreement or consensus on the decisions. However, so far no survey has asked questions specifically related to how and at what stages these managers get involved, so we still have an incomplete picture of this aspect of the SID process.

Based on our analysis of the literature, including at least 16 case studies, covering over 300 SIDs, we propose a basic model of the SID process as a point of departure for this study. We aim to explore the potential link between the number of participating managers and the scope for the psychological aspects of managerial judgement and the use of decision support systems to encourage consensus. There is a need for research on SIDs to explore both the individual and collective role of managerial judgement rather than to focus on the way individuals make decisions.

The role of managerial judgement in SIDs

Herbert Simon's work on decision-making processes in administrative organisation spans over 50 years. Midway through this period, in 1978, he was awarded a Nobel Prize in Economics for his theory of bounded rationality. Whilst most economics-based research on SIDs assumed that decision-makers act rationally, Simon (1957) identified three models of behaviour or types of rationality. First, 'economic man' is assumed to have all relevant information and a complete and consistent system of preferences, as well as the ability to perform complex probability calculations to produce economically optimal solutions.

Second, 'social man' is more attuned to human issues and introduces an acknowledgement of self-interest and the role that reward has to play in influencing managerial decisions, admitting the 'agency' issue to the model. Third, 'administrative man' is driven by expediency and a desire to complete sufficient analysis, but only until a satisfactory outcome is found, acknowledging 'satisficing' behaviour, where the complexities of the real world are simplified and prioritised. 'Administrative man' may therefore be influenced by concepts of market share, fair price and adequate rather than optimal profits.

Simon (1976), in his introduction to the third edition of 'Administrative Behaviour', extends earlier notions of the limits of rationality to consider the psychological and organisational influences on choice more fully. He identified the personal preferences for continuity and completion that influence managerial judgement, e.g. resistance to abort projects even when sunk costs are irrelevant, referred to as 'status quo bias' (Samuelson and Zeckhauser, 1988) and 'escalating commitment' (Staw, 1981). Simon (1976, p. xxxiv) states "My present inclination would be to stress the cognitive factors a good deal more". Many later researchers have picked up on the problems of goal incongruence and information asymmetry (Haka, 2007), but not all of Simon's insights have been followed up in subsequent research.

Strategic cognition plays a very important role in the diagnosis of strategic issues and formulation of problems (Schwenk, 1988). In business the concept of intuitive decision-making causes people's view to be polarised more than any other concepts. Intuitive judgement has been defined by Kahneman and Tversky (1982, p. 124) as judgement reached through "an informal and unstructured mode of reasoning, without the use of analytic methods or deliberate calculation". In other words, it is not based on lots of facts and figures but the bright ideas arising from people's hunches (Emery, 2002). Salton (2000) has pointed out that people are uncomfortable with intuition as a decision-making strategy since they find it very difficult to process information without all the facts. Nevertheless, managers need to apply a blend of logic and intuition (what Emery, *op. cit.*, refers to as 'whole-brain thinking') to help their organisations find the way around today's uncharted business territory within which SIDs take place.

To summarise from the review of earlier studies, we conclude that managerial judgement can play an important role in SIDs. Figure 1.2 shows the base model of the SID process that guided this research and specifically influenced the questions used in this survey.

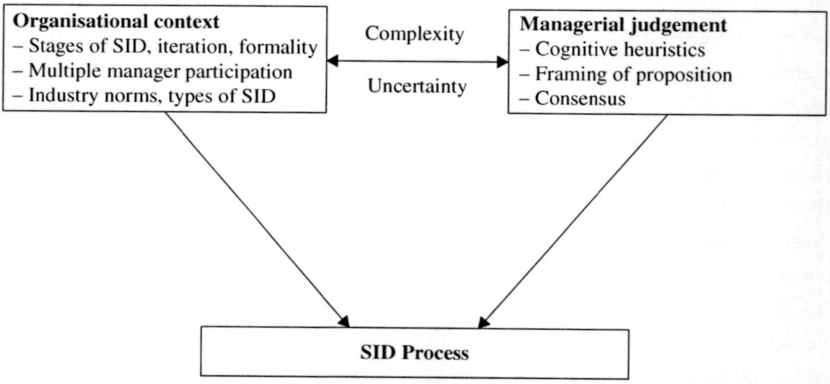

Figure 1.2 Base model of the SID process

Summary

This chapter has given an overview of the literature on SIDs, highlighting the key factors in the organisational context in which the SID process takes place, stages in the SID process and the potential for psychological phenomenon to influence managerial judgement. The role that managerial judgement plays in the SID process has been explored by case-based researchers, but has never been the focus for a cross-sectional survey, until now. It is this focus and the key concepts in understanding managerial judgement that we explain in the next chapter.

Chapter 2

Managerial Judgement

Introduction

This chapter narrows the scope of the literature review, from the overview of SIDs given in the previous chapter to explain the key factors that influence managerial judgement in SIDs, which provides the focus for this research. It defines the key terms, heuristics, framing and consensus in the everyday language of management accountants used in the design of the survey questions in this study.

Managers' strategic cognition and psychological concepts

The work of Simon (1957, 1976), Staw (1981), Schwenk (1988) and Kahneman and Tversky (1982) provided the background theories to suggest that managers' strategic cognition and key psychological concepts are worthy of further investigation. Hastie and Dawes (2001) have updated and added insights to the body of knowledge on the psychology of judgement in decision-making. There are many aspects that could usefully be investigated, but we select three concepts for this research, which are broad enough to capture most relevant behaviours previously identified.

The investigation of three main themes (heuristics, framing and consensus), potentially important in exercising managerial judgement in SIDs, is informed by the cognitive psychology and organisational behaviour literature. The first, *heuristics*, deals with the psychological influences on judgement under uncertainty (Tversky and Kahneman, 1974). The second, *framing*, is another form of cognitive bias which is observed when decision-makers react differently to the same basic information presented or framed in a different way (Tversky and Kahneman, 1986). The third, *consensus*, deals with group dynamics, and the ad hoc ways in which managers seek to influence others (Pettigrew, 1973) in the decision-making process (Mintzberg et al., 1976; Schweiger et al., 1986). This third concept draws more from organisational studies on the behaviour of managers, so combines psychological, sociological and political perspectives.

Heuristics

Heuristics is the *application of experience-derived knowledge to a problem*, i.e. the use of heuristic. Heuristic is derived from the Greek word *heuriskein*, which means *to discover*, and it is basically a *rule of thumb*, or *commonsense rule(s)*, or *line of reasoning* derived from experience and intended to increase the chances of solving a problem. It pertains to the process of acquisition of knowledge by intelligent guesswork rather than by following some pre-established procedure. Behavioural decision theory has evidence that cognitive heuristics and biases influence strategic decision-making (Gilovich et al., 2002; Schwenk, 1988, 1984; Slovic et al., 1977; Tversky and Kahneman, 1974).

Simon (1957, 1976) suggests that since strategic decision problems are complex and decision-makers have cognitive limitations, there is need for simplification of the problems; inevitably in the process of such simplification, heuristics and biases may prevail. Similarly, Tversky and Kahneman (1974) recognised that heuristics and biases are employed by decision-makers, when making decisions under conditions of uncertainty.

Decision-makers simplify a complex problem by applying a rule of thumb instead of using a sophisticated mathematical model to solve the problem. Kahneman and Tversky's (1974) research revealed that decision-makers use heuristics, based on their own knowledge and experience, and evaluate new opportunities by comparing them with a reference point from personal knowledge. The process is known as *anchoring* and *adjustment*. In this case the decision-maker would make estimates by reference to an initial value (*the anchor*) and then add or subtract an *adjustment* to indicate new information.

An example of this approach in management accounting is the use of incremental budgeting, where estimates for future costs may be based on what was spent or budgeted for last year, plus or minus a sum or percentage to take account of changing conditions, e.g. inflation. Whilst this approach is much maligned in the accountancy literature, with more advocates for a zero-based budgeting approach, or even beyond budgeting forms of control, there are cases where incremental approaches may be acceptable based on a low level of predicted change in the planning period, and therefore it may even become a formal method. A similar argument may be used in capital budgeting, if an organisation is investing routinely in projects of a similar type, such that anchoring and adjustment may be appropriate. However, most writers on decision theory regard these heuristics as undesirable in a process of rational choice as they may ignore important new information.

Recent research has cautioned that there may be a considerable difference in the effectiveness of anchoring and adjustment between situations where the decision-takers generate their own anchors and those where suitable anchors are provided in initial project information (Epley and Gilovich, 2002). An example of organisationally generated anchors in SIDs may be the use of cost estimation models based on past project costs and drivers, typical in the pharmaceutical industry for evaluating research and development projects. Despite limitations of using such anchor values, they may prove more valuable than self-generated anchors.

There is also a view that a more recently identified *affect* heuristic should replace *anchoring* in the judgement of risks and benefits in decision-making (Slovic et al., 2000). This is defined as an emotive cognitive response to a problem or decision which occurs before any more complete reasoning process takes place, by which we decide whether we are positively or negatively disposed to an option (Bazerman, 2006). Whilst this is described as a heuristic, it has so much to do with how options are presented, that it could fit better within our concept of framing, as described below.

Decision-makers also have a tendency to classify their knowledge and recall events which represent those of similar type: the heuristics of *representativeness*. There are accepted statistical techniques for ascertaining how representative a sample of data might be of the population, but human information processing, even by scientists, tends to bypass such computations and uses intuition in place of computation (Tversky and Kahneman, 1971). The intuitive response to an initial project opportunity may be fast, almost automatic, using a process of prototype or stereotype recognition. The types of SID set out in Box 1.2 could provide this sort of prompt either by giving managers this information about a new project opportunity or relying on their past experience of similar projects to make this cognitive connection. Kahneman and Frederick (2002: 51) distinguish this intuitive cognitive system from that of a more reflective system of reason characterised by a more self-aware application of rules in a deductive or controlled way.

The *availability* of experience to use as a reference point may also influence decision-makers' judgement. In most case-based studies of SIDs, managers have been observed to have significant past experience of similar decisions to be able to recall project attributes. However, sometimes the level of past experience of projects of a certain type or opportunities in a certain industry can lead to *overconfidence* when assessing new projects, which is why assumptions should be questioned and challenged in a systematic way in reaching group-based decisions (Bazerman, 2006). Bazerman (2006) recognised extensions to this group of concepts to include the emotional 'affect' heuristic. He also developed Simon's notions of bounded rationality further, introducing 'bounded awareness'.

Framing of propositions

This concept is closely related to the concept of heuristics and postulates that decision-makers react differently to the same basic information *presented* or *framed* in a different way (Tversky and Kahneman, 1986). This relates to personal expectations and preferences and the decision-maker's attitude to risk. An example of a personal preference that often conflicts with economic rational analysis is that of preferring the status quo compared to significant change (Samuelson and Zeckhauser, 1988). The term *status quo bias* is used to describe the phenomenon of using the status quo or 'do nothing' option as a preference in decision analysis. Tversky and Kahneman (1991) in their study on reference dependence explored this dimension further, though as the study focused on consumer choice, it added little to our knowledge of SIDs. This bias could be grouped with heuristics or framing, but as it is a response to a proposition based on personal preference, we regard it as a framing effect.

The role, which bias in framing plays in strategic decisions, continues to attract the attention of academics and practitioners alike. Hodgkinson et al. (1999) conducted a field-based empirical investigation into the use of causal cognitive maps in strategic decisions in order to examine whether such use might reduce the effect of framing bias. They found that cognitive mapping (described later in this chapter under the section 'Consensus') prior to choice did reduce bias. However, more work is needed in this area to support the prescriptive validity of their findings that cognitive mapping improves the quality of strategic decisions.

Tversky and Kahneman (1986) looked at the impact which the framing of prospects (i.e. definition and description of the opportunities) had on the evaluation phase of the decision and therefore the ultimate choice. They carried out many studies and found that decision-makers placed more emphasis on the initial information about the choice (which is termed *primacy*), or on the most recent information (which is termed *recency*), rather than taking a balanced view of all the data. The influence of primacy and recency in the human processing of information made an important contribution.

However, the importance attached to the information relating to a decision may be influenced by self-interest, thus primacy of information varies between individuals as well as over time. Individuals also have a tendency to recall examples from the recent past more readily than from the distant past, and to place more importance upon recent or up-to-date information. Reactions to proposals also draw quite heavily on the emotive or intuitive (right) side of the brain; a process that tends to happen subconsciously in even the most ethical and conscientious managers (Claxton, 1998; Holloman, 1992).

Collective decision-making and group processes

In the organisational context in which SIDs take place, individuals rarely identify, evaluate and decide upon strategic investments in isolation from others, with the possible exception of a small business owner who is a sole trader with no other interested parties. Therefore the participation of organisational members and related parties in the making of strategic decisions introduces the issue of group behaviour and the view that some degree of consensus is necessary to agree SIDs. The effectiveness of those group processes has been investigated from a variety of perspectives. The value of group decision-making is recognised by Hall (1971, p. 51) who observed that: 'Group decisions often are frustrating and inadequate. All members want agreement, but they also want to make their own points heard'. The net result, however, could be a group decision which outperforms the average of individuals' decision-making.

On the other hand, Janis (1982) examines the danger of 'group think' where familiarity cushions in-group managers from alternative views and paradigms. Hillson and Murray-Webster (2005, pp. 71–75) draw attention to three more group behaviours. The 'Moses Factor' is where members of the group adopt the risk preference of an influential and charismatic leader, allowing the leader's views to dominate the discussion and influence the outcome of the SID. 'Cultural conformity' is where organisational culture has an undue or hidden influence on the SID, such that decisions fit with the perceived ethos or values of the organisation. After sharing individual views, the group risk attitude can 'shift' to become more (cautious shift) or less (risky shift) risk averse.

Consensus therefore draws attention to group composition and the dynamic interaction, or otherwise, of the group members. The ad hoc ways in which managers seek to influence others (Pettigrew, 1973) and the various means of seeking consensus (Schweiger et al., 1986) are also pertinent to understanding decision-making involving multiple managers. There has been useful research from social and political science perspectives which highlights the importance of group identity, by observing solidarity and universal promising in dilemma situations (Dawes et al., 1988). This socio-political dimension of decision-making has been observed in field studies on capital budgeting (Bower, 1986; Hickson et al., 1986; Lumijärvi, 1991; Mintzberg et al., 1976).

Consensus

Consensus is defined as the group process of sharing interpretations of the proposal and its assumptions in reaching agreement as to the decision. The number of groups and individuals consulted or involved in the SID in some way will naturally increase the propensity for more group behaviour to influence the final decision. The effect can be both positive (to collect more views from a variety of perspectives) in ensuring final commitment to a project, and negative (if any party is unduly privileged by the decision).

The detection of group behaviour has been possible through case studies. Bower (1986) and Lumijärvi (1991, p. 176) found evidence of project champions canvassing support for their project and negotiating it up through the hierarchy of an organisation, giving the project 'impetus'. Hickson et al. (1986, p. 238) found evidence of 'politicality' and managerial pluralism of interests. Mintzberg et al. (1976) identified intense political activity in several cases, including evidence of coalitions formed to protect common interests. Managers may not agree upon every aspect of the proposal, but SID procedures usually allow some form of cognitive consensus to be reached (Mohammed, 2001).

Eden (1989) introduced a cognitive mapping technique in Strategic Options Development and Analysis (SODA) to help managers form a diagrammatical representation of their group thinking on a strategic option, which has been widely used in the strategy field (Huff and Jenkins, 2002). Whilst cognitive mapping can be perceived as a group or consensus process, more managers may have come across mind maps as an individual heuristic.

Summary

This brief review of the cognitive psychology and organisational behaviour literature suggests that the three themes, heuristics, framing and consensus, are potentially important in exercising managerial judgement, and they are possible keys to unlocking the puzzle of human behaviour during SIDs. These themes, summarised in Box 2.1, have strongly influenced the design of the research instrument (analytic survey questionnaire) for this study.

BOX 2.1 KEY CONCEPTS IN MANAGERIAL JUDGEMENT

- Heuristics – a set of simplifying means by which managers draw on their knowledge, experience, values and beliefs in forming intuitive judgements under conditions of uncertainty. They include:
  - Representativeness – categorising of projects of similar type
  - Availability – reference to industry norms and benchmarks
  - Anchoring and adjustment – use of base values and increments
  - Mind maps or mental pictures
- Framing – the way managers respond differently to the same proposition depending upon how the decision information is presented or framed, due to personal preferences that may bias the human processing of information. This set of preferences may include:
  - Primacy – more emphasis on initial information
  - Recency – more emphasis on the most recent information
  - Status quo bias – preference for continuity or aversion to change
  - Risk preference – risk averse or risk seeking attitude to risk
- Consensus – the way managers share and exchange views about potential projects in group decision-making processes, both formally (e.g. through management team or board meetings) and informally (e.g. through corridor conversations and emails). Processes may include:
  - Consultation – with stakeholder groups in or external to the organisation
  - Canvassing – a project champion campaigning for support, negotiating the project up through the hierarchy to ensure its acceptance and approval
  - Coalitions – joining forces with like-minded individuals to protect common interests

Chapter 3

Survey Design

Introduction

Management accounting literature has largely moved from survey-based to case-based research, with the recent exception of a CIMA-sponsored survey on risk management practices (Collier et al., 2007). The psychology of choice and judgement in decision-making literature is dominated by experimental research, which ignores the organisational context in which corporate decisions are made. The rationale for a survey to be used in this research is that whilst numerous capital budgeting surveys have been conducted in the past, the emphasis has been on the techniques used in practice in the evaluation stage of the SID process. None have focused upon human behaviour and the role of managerial judgement in organisations in the context of the broader SID process.

This chapter describes the design of the analytic survey questionnaire and how the literature reviewed in Chapters 1 and 2 influenced the framing of the questions. It also sets out the survey administration process, the characteristics of the target sample and respondents in terms of the industry classification of companies, and the process and methods of data analysis. The questionnaire is reproduced in Appendix 1 and the results are analysed in the next chapter.

The analytic survey questionnaire

A 32-item questionnaire (Appendix 1) was developed to find evidence of managerial involvement and the psychological themes and further explanations of the SID process. A summary of the conceptual derivation of the questions from the themes identified in Chapters 1 and 2 is shown in Table 3.1, and are grouped as follows:

- context and types of SIDs
- managerial involvement
- stages in and nature of the SID process
- heuristics, framing and consensus questions

Context and types of SID questions

These questions on organisational context, industry class, job title/role, types of SIDs and years of experience were incorporated as questions 1 to 9 of the questionnaire. Experience is critical in the positive application of heuristics, intuition and response to data presented, so question 20 was included to identify the nature of knowledge and experience that was considered important in influencing SIDs. Arguably, the context of SIDs is under-researched in management accounting literature and the inclusion of these questions should provide new insights into the context of SIDs. Question 31 was included to confirm that examples selected by respondents followed a typical SID process in their company.

Managerial involvement

The extent of managerial involvement was ascertained in question 10 and the nature of that involvement was explored in questions 11 to 17. An opportunity was given for managers to suggest improvements to their own organisation's practice in question 32, producing valuable information for both the organisations and to CIMA members.

Questions on stages in and the nature of the SID process

This group includes question 10 on stages of the SID process, question 29 on company practice and procedures in SIDs and question 30 on the use of decision support software (DSS). It was recognised that different organisations might have different SID processes, thus the questions aimed to cast more light on such differences as well as to confirm the stages identified in Box 1.1. Question 32 gave respondents the opportunity to recommend improvements to the SID process in their company, which may reveal which aspects are not regarded as areas of good practice. Areas of weakness may also be useful for other organisations to benchmark.

Heuristics questions

In this group, questions 18 and 19 were designed to discover the use of heuristics, without actually using that term, which may not be considered everyday language.

Table 3.1 Summary of the conceptual themes in the questionnaire

Themes from the literature	Evidence collected by survey question
Context and types of SID	
Company name (for industry classification)	1
Job title	2
Professional background and work experience	3 to 7 and 20
Types of SID experienced and focus for survey	8, 9 and 31
Stages in and nature of the SID process	
Stages	10
Requirements of company procedures	29
Use of decision support software (DSS)	30
Improvements recommended	32
Multiple manager involvement in SID process	
Involvement of internal managers in SIDs	11 and 12
Involvement of external managers in SIDs	13 to 15
Nature of involvement	16 and 17
Heuristics	
Use of intuitive processes and rules of thumb	18
Use of base values and tolerance ranges (anchoring and adjustment) and experience of similar projects	19
Intuition vs. evaluation in risk assessment	28
Framing	
Response to up-to-date information (recency)	21
What sort of information proved problematic	22
What sources of information were available to access	23
Consensus	
Socio-political processes, e.g. lobbying	24
How group processes influenced own views	25
Group behaviour	26
Important factors in reaching agreement	27

More familiar terms such as gut feeling or hunches, mental pictures, brainstorming and rules of thumb in SIDs were used. How new project opportunities are compared to previous examples was explored to provide evidence on the availability and representativeness of relevant knowledge and experience during the process. In addition, the use of stereotypes to classify projects; industry and other benchmarks and base value and tolerance ranges to evaluate projects might be crucial to provide evidence of anchoring and adjustment as part of managerial judgement in SIDs. Question 28 sought to establish the balance between intuitive and analytical approaches to risk assessment in the SID process.

Framing questions

Questions 21 to 23 were included on the nature of information available and the influence of how that information is presented on managerial judgement in the SIDs. These questions explored the possible sources of framing bias in the SID process and what sort of new or additional information might change the respondents' view of the project under consideration (recency).

Consensus questions

This group included questions 24 to 27 on the use of various group approaches in the SID examples selected by respondents. They explore how consensus was achieved during the process and the importance of Kelly's constructs of commonality and sociality (Kelly, 1955) and managers' experience in attaining consensus in SID. How SID teams were formed (including formation of ad hoc teams, coalitions, negotiation and alliance-building) and their composition would provide more insight into the role of consensus in the process. Moreover, the impact of the socio-political process of canvassing support from top management might be evidenced. These questions were linked to those on managerial involvement, e.g. questions 13 to 16 on external consultation.

The following types of question were included in the questionnaire in order to introduce variety, which would make the questionnaire more interesting for various respondents in different job roles to complete and enrich the quality of the responses:

- Questions with options
- Closed (Yes/No) questions
- 5-point Likert scale questions (with a 6th not applicable option)
- Open questions

Table 3.1 summarises the links between the themes identified in Chapters 1 and 2 and the questions asked in the survey instrument.

Pilot testing

The draft questionnaire was pre-tested with a group of management students to ensure that respondents would understand the questions and be able to answer them within a reasonable time. The draft instrument was also presented at a Management Control conference to elicit feedback on the framing of questions from academics. Minor changes were made to both the wording of questions and to the labelling of the rating scales as a result.

The researchers assured individual respondents of confidentiality; ensured that the survey was short, interesting and easy to complete; carefully ordered the questions (using mutually exclusive and exhaustive response categories for the Likert scale questions); requested the respondents to base their responses on the most recent SID they have been involved with; used reverse-scored items and provided a 'Not Applicable' option. The use of jargon and emotionally charged words was avoided; giving justification for the questions; and using a counter-biasing statement when wording the questions. The questions were made clear, precise and relatively short. Leading and double-barrelled questions were also avoided: similarly, double negatives were also avoided when the questions were constructed.

The sample and distribution of the questionnaire

Sampling

Initially companies from 29 industry sectors (using the Financial Times Sector Categorisation) were selected. A list of all 1,189 companies listed on the London Stock Exchange in these sectors was drawn up. The list of companies was sent to CIMA to identify their members working in those companies. Members with senior job titles were selected as those most likely to have knowledge and experience of SIDs in their organisations, and were targeted as potential respondents. CIMA provided the researchers with a list of 2,379 such members working in 416 of the listed companies. Those 416 companies became the target sample of companies investigated. Table 3.2 shows the number of companies represented by the responses, spread across the industry sectors.

Table 3.2 Summary of respondents

	Sector	Companies in sector	Companies targeted	Companies in sample	Individual responses
A	Aerospace and Defence	13	7	2	5
B	Automobile and Parts	19	9	2	3
C	Beverages	9	6	3	6
D	Chemicals	20	8	1	1
E	Construction and Building Materials	74	44	11	12
F	Diversified Industries	5	3	0	0
G	Electricity	7	3	0	0
H	Electronic and Electrical	43	18	5	5
I	Food and Drug Retailers	12	7	1	1
J	Food Producers and Processors	29	8	2	2
K	Forestry and Paper	4	1	0	0
L	Healthcare	37	12	2	2
M	Household Goods and Textiles	50	18	0	0
N	IT Hardware	30	14	1	1

O	Leisure Hotels	84	26	2	2
P	Media Entertainment	115	29	2	2
Q	Mining	29	6	1	1
R	Oil Gas	31	7	2	3
S	Other utilities	12	5	3	4
T	Personal Care Household	7	6	1	2
U	Pharmaceuticals Biotech	44	10	2	4
V	Real Estate	78	11	2	2
W	Retailers General	72	26	3	3
X	Software Services	139	48	2	2
Y	Steel Other Metals	3	1	1	4
Z	Support Services	160	54	7	11
AA	Telecom Services	20	10	4	5
AB	Tobacco	3	1	0	0
AC	Transport	40	18	3	8
	Total	1,189	416	65	91

Distribution of questionnaires

The researchers initially planned to use email distribution. The use of electronic mail and online facilities was initially expected to be less costly in terms of time and money; yield faster returns; and give respondents the time to answer the questions at their convenience, as noted by Mangione (1995) and Tse (1998). The questionnaire was designed and installed on the De Montfort University website and access and submission processes tested.

However, the researchers experienced two problems with the online method. First, the CIMA database available at the time did not contain email addresses for a large number of members. Second, there was a big problem of non-response. For the first batch of emails sent to more than 300 members working in three of the largest companies, there was not a single usable response (despite the system having been confirmed as live and working). Thus it was agreed to change the method of distribution to a conventional postal delivery.

Postal survey

When the online questionnaire failed to deliver any responses, the analytical survey questionnaires were delivered through the post and returned using self-addressed prepaid envelopes. The postal delivery was coupled with the option of filling out the questionnaire online, if this was preferable. Just 4 of the 91 respondents chose to do so. The questionnaires were coded to assist with the follow-up of non-responses. The delivery was batched, with the first postal batch consisting of 1,000 questionnaires posted to the CIMA members in companies excluding the 3 contacted by email. This was followed up after 2 weeks by email and by telephone, where the telephone numbers were traceable. When the researchers started receiving responses from this method, indicating a much better response rate, the remaining questionnaires (including a repeat of the first 300 members in the first three companies initially contacted by email) were dispatched.

Response bias

The researchers put respondent profile questions into the design of the questionnaire to control for response bias brought about by the orientation or biases of the respondents. However, since it was the individual perspectives of the managers being investigated, the sectors and company profiles may not significantly affect the results of the study. Table 3.2 shows the spread of responses across sectors, which is fairly evenly spread. Only five sectors were not represented in the responses, three of which were very small.

Respondents

Responses

All the responses received were dated, numbered and filed according to the company code that had been attached to each (to ease identification of cases of non-response to follow up). The responses were categorised upon receipt:

- return to sender (where the respondents were no longer with the companies) 172
- respondents not willing to participate in the study 11
- respondents not qualified to participate in the study 7
- usable responses 91

The 91 usable responses were from individual respondents in 65 companies. The company response rate was 16% (65/416). Of the 29 sectors originally identified, Table 3.2 shows responses from the 65 companies covered 24 sectors, so fulfils the aims of a broad cross-sectional survey. The individual profile of respondents, in terms of their job titles, seniority, experience and involvement in the SID process is analysed at the beginning of Chapter 4.

Data analysis

The survey responses were first analysed using descriptive statistics, for questions with yes/no or option answers (questions 3 to 16, 21, 24 and 30); these are shown as percentages in Appendix 2. The answers to open questions (questions 17 and 32, and the 'others please specify' elements of option questions) were analysed using content analysis. The themes resulting from question 17 are shown in Appendix 2, but to keep this summary brief the results from question 32 are analysed in a separate table in Chapter 4.

The answers to questions 18 to 20 and 22, 23, 25 to 29, and 31 were categorised into the 5-point scale or not applicable, making six categories. These were first analysed in terms of a mean score and standard deviation, where 3 would be the mean expected if the responses followed a normal distribution (Appendix 3). Mean scores of above 3 indicate a greater than average incidence of the variable observed. An overall level of support (OLS) was also calculated by adding together the percentage of responses in categories 3 to 5, 'on average to great extent'. All percentages have been rounded to one decimal place in Appendix 2, and are rounded to whole percentages in the discussion in this report.

Where there was a likely explanation for variation in scores in one question to be found in the variation in scores to another, e.g. a possible link between heuristics used and the type of project selected by the respondent, a contingency table was constructed and a chi-squared value calculated to establish any significant link. Where significant links were found, these tables appear in Chapter 4, with the contributing factors highlighted.

Factor analysis was also used to explore possible relationships between the variables in the data set. This revealed very little of significance to add to the findings but informed the case study analysis in Appendix 4.

Summary

The survey resulted in 91 usable responses spread across 65 companies in 24 industries, which gives us a sufficient sample from which to gain insights into SID practice in a reasonable number of UK companies, with a unique emphasis on the behaviourial aspects of managerial judgement and the context within with SIDs are made. Results of the survey are discussed in Chapter 4.

Chapter 4

Survey Analysis

Introduction

This chapter contains the analysis of the survey responses, starting with a section on the profile of respondents. It then divides the results into four aspects of the SID context, types of SID, stages in and nature of the SID process and manager involvement in the process, followed by the three psychological themes (heuristics, framing and consensus). The next chapter discusses the implications of these findings from a number of stakeholder perspectives.

Respondent profiles

There were 91 usable responses from CIMA members working in 65 companies. The industry analysis was set out in Table 3.2, showing the spread of responses across 24 industries. In this section, we examine responses to questions 2 to 7 of the questionnaire, concerning the job title, background and experience of respondents. Table 4.1 shows the analysis of job titles.

A content analysis of the job titles revealed 10 with accountant in the title, 42 with finance or financial and 3 with other accounting and finance-related titles, making a total of 55 accounting and finance specialists. There were 32 respondents with director in their title including 21 finance directors. There were 6 CEOs, 1 chairman, 3 MDs, 8 other directors and 4 vice presidents amongst the senior

Table 4.1 Analysis of respondent job titles

Level of seniority	**Accounting and finance specialists**	**General management roles**	**Total**
High level Chief accountant, chief finance officer, finance director, group treasurer, chairman, CEO, director, MD, vice president	25	22	47
Others included: Accountant, analyst, financial controller, finance manager, general manager, development manager, value stream leader	30	14	44
Total	55	36	91

general management roles. Whilst all respondents were in fairly senior roles, over half were in more senior roles using the above definitions.

The most frequently used job titles amongst the less senior roles were 11 financial controllers, and 8 people who simply described themselves as managers. A high proportion (81%) of respondents had been in their current position for 5 years or less, but 75% had worked in the same company for 6 or more years, which shows that many CIMA members had changed job titles in recent years, most probably through promotion. Whilst 23 people had worked in the same company for 5 years or less, there were 36 people who had worked in similar positions in other companies before joining their current company.

Types of projects

Question 8 asked about which types of project respondents had experience of, and question 9 asked which specific type of SID they would focus on to answer the rest of the questions. Table 4.2 shows the frequency of project types for these two questions with the most common project types experienced listed first. Question 31 confirmed that the SID process, for example, used as the focus for the survey was

Table 4.2 Project types

Type of project in your SID experience	Experienced		Focus
	Count	%	%
New technology or infrastructure, e.g. computer systems projects	64	70	18
New site or site development (new location, relocation, expansion)	62	68	21
Acquisitions of business assets or companies	55	60	26
New product development	43	47	14
Other, e.g. decommissioning, downsizing, business process design	42	46	9
New market development (new customers/ clients)	38	42	11
Compliance (new legislation, e.g. health and safety)	31	34	1
Total (for n = 91 respondents)			100

highly typical in terms of using normal procedures in the organisation for 94% of cases (only 1 case was not typical at all).

The respondents exhibit wide experience of a range of SID projects as shown by the percentage in the second column in Table 4.2. It can be seen that the three most common types of project experienced by respondents in SID-making in their organisations were also the most commonly selected examples (in column 3) for the rest of the survey (chosen by 65% of respondents), though acquisitions were the most frequently selected type of projects and could also be viewed as the most strategic.

Stages in the SID process

Question 10 asked respondents to say which of the 10 stages identified in the SID process (Box 1.1) applied in their company and at which stages they were personally involved. Table 4.3 shows there is strong support (74–98%) to confirm the 10 stages in the SID process. This question also allowed for other stages not listed to be identified. There were 15 responses to 'other, please specify', which have been analysed as either equivalent to stated stages (4) or new (11 responses). The two new stages identified in this question were:

1. Implementation and testing (9 people)
2. Change management (3 people including 1 who also identified implementation)

Table 4.3 Applicable stages in the SID process and managerial involvement at each stage

Stages in the SID process	Applicable in company (%)	Senior-level managers (%)	Lower-level managers (%)
1. Scanning for project opportunities	76	40	36
2. Defining projects/ formulating options	89	66	57
3. Generation of project data	82	53	64
4. Making preliminary assumptions	92	68	57
5. Early screening discussion on project	87	68	64
6. Estimation of cash flow/ financial data	98	74	77
7. Formal evaluation of the project (DCF)	82	60	73
8. Progression through the company, persuading senior managers to support the project	91	68	80
9. Authorisation of the project	91	68	39
10. Post-audit evaluation (project review)	74	49	48
+Other stages			
– implementation and testing	10		
– managing change	3		

There is a high level of involvement (over 58%) of respondents in 7 of the stages (2nd to 8th). There is somewhat less involvement (39%) in stage 1 in scanning for opportunities, in authorisation (54%), post-audit (48%) and the two new stages (13%), though some involvement is still apparent.

The respondents' involvement seems to pervade the entire process with a concentration on the middle stages where financial data may be used. This is consistent with the roles reflected in the job titles of respondents in Table 4.1, as 60% have specialist financial jobs and 40% have broader managerial jobs. The level of involvement has been analysed by the level of seniority taken from Table 4.1. Where this differs significantly by level the percentage is highlighted in Table 4.3.

It can be seen that more senior managers are more likely to be involved in stages 4 and 9, shaping the project outline and authorising the project, and less senior managers are more likely to be involved in stages 3, 7 and 8, the data generation and analysis and persuasion.

Table 4.4 Question 29 Formal company requirements for SID procedures

Does your company require	Mean*	Standard deviation
A set of standard procedures (e.g. procedures manual) to be employed	3.32	1.54
Assumptions underlying your decision to be stated	4.30	0.88
Top management's approval	4.73	0.54
Dissenting opinions to be reported	2.56	1.37
An individual manager to champion and be responsible for the SID	3.97	1.24

**1 = hardly at all, 5 = to a great extent and 0 = not applicable.*

Nature of the SID process

Table 4.4 reveals that most respondents' organisations require a set of standard procedures to be employed, e.g. following a procedures manual or standard instructions for SIDs. Appendix 2 shows that there were 7 respondents who said not at all and another 7 who said hardly at all, though there were no responses with scores of 0 or 1 for requiring top management approval.

Only 3 respondents answered 0 or 1 for assumptions underlying the decision were required to be stated (97% OLS); 91% scored 3 to 5 for having an individual manager as project champion responsible for the SID. However, only 52% scored 3 to 5 for reporting dissenting opinions. This is an interesting finding, as some of the consensus seeking activities seem to encourage the 'challenging of project assumptions' and 'devil's advocacy', but it may go unreported even if unresolved.

In question 30 on decision support systems, 90% use spreadsheet models to aid project appraisal, which is unsurprising; 51% use critical path analysis to manage projects, which shows the widespread availability of project management software in companies today. Just 4% use specific decision support packages, but 18% use decision trees. Only 6% use no decision support software at all.

Thirty-eight respondents answered question 32 which called for suggestions to improve the SID-making process in their organisations. Of the 38 replies to this question, 8 respondents call for more than one improvement in their SID processes and 6 identified at least 3 areas of weakness. Only one respondent (a CEO of a company in the construction and building materials industry) thought his organisation's process required no change at all, stating 'Combination of financial modelling within a predetermined strategic framework has served us well over a number of years'. In contrast, a management accountant in a major retail company suggested four areas for improvement just for site acquisition type projects.

Of the 37 responses suggesting improvements, a total of 59 suggestions have been analysed. Tables 4.5 (a)–(e) show extracts from the text for 53 of the suggestions made, split between the five main project types. A content analysis of the full 59 suggestions reveals 25 focus on process issues (10 on the stages or need for compliance, 10 on timing, 3 on post-completion reviews and 2 on change management), 15 on consensus issues (including wider consultations with interested parties, calls for clearer communications and improved political processes), 14 on framing issues (more information evaluated including sensitivity analysis and risk analysis), and 5 on heuristics (including 3 who call for greater use of 'gut feel' and intuition and 2 who call for less bureaucracy or formality).

Managerial involvement

Ninety-eight per cent have formal meetings within the company to discuss SIDs (Q11). Other (non-financial) managers involved in these formal meetings (Q12) were business development managers (49%), finance managers (81%), marketing managers (29%), IT managers (40%), operations managers (59%), project managers (61%) and production managers (28%).

A majority (64%) also indicated their organisations hold meetings with external parties (questions 13 to 15), including 39% with consultants, 30% with suppliers, 16% with customers, 16% with financiers and 15% with government departments.

Table 4.5a New product development projects ($n = 9$ respondents, total 13 suggestions)

Industry sector	Comments/suggestions
Pharmaceuticals	More use of 'gut feel' and intuition Need to streamline/speed up product launch stage
Beverages	More involvement from supply in innovation projects Faster roll-outs to other markets Flexible stage-gate process tailored to individual projects
Support services	Greater clarity about end objective More structured timetable for project Awareness of key deadlines Ensure it is well thought through, then sleep on it!
Construction	Process review to consider all aspects and individual roles
Aerospace	Realistic timeline from the outset
Media and entertainment	Greater assistance from directors to tackle political issues NPD can be time critical, 24 months and 13 board presentations too long!

Table 4.5b New market development projects ($n = 5$ respondents, total 8 suggestions)

Industry sector	Comments/suggestions
Transport	Personal influences and functional input have too much impact Formal structure used but not trusted or respected More speed through smaller management committees Greater gut feel impact on decision-making
Support services	More open communication and goal congruence
Chemicals	Ensure rigorous evaluation of opportunities Transparent communication of key issues to decision-makers
Telecoms	Robust process used, though occasionally too process driven

Table 4.5c New site projects (n = 6 respondents, total 13 suggestions)

Industry sector	Comments/suggestions
Steel and other metals	Clear definition of strategic company objectives Competitor benchmarking – cost of production, etc. Shorter decision-making time
Retail	Thoroughly consider location ABC analysis Size of build to fit above factors (to maximise ROI) Consider potential impact of competitors' movements
Beverages	Better post completion audits/learning and accountability
Support services	Make non-financial staff more aware of benefits of SID
Real estate	Identification of all interested parties earlier in the project Longer planning time Project should not be led by CEO Project leader should have wide business experience, not necessarily technical background

Table 4.5d New technology projects (n = 7 respondents, total 9 suggestions)

Industry sector	Comments/suggestions
Aerospace	Ensure everyone follows process
Utilities	Needs to be less bureaucratic Operational priorities frequently delay decision-making Rationalisation changed purpose and rules in the middle of the SID
Support services	Wider range of opinions and experiences to be brought into process
Electronics	More formalised process to evaluate planning and achievement of targets More emphasis on sensitivity analysis – review effect of changing assumptions
Retail	More evaluation of risk Greater testing/challenging of scenarios

Table 4.5e Business acquisition projects ($n = 7$ respondents, total 10 suggestions)

Industry sector	Comments/suggestions
Steel and other metals	Open to as wide scrutiny as possible, realising people have vested interests
Support services	Post-implementation reviews to pass learning to next SID Greater use of business modelling Better planning of post-acquisition HR activity Improve communications before, during and after
Construction	Process needs to be shortened Less formality/checklists, more concentration on future prospects Allocate resources more effectively, so individuals not managing SID and the day job for prolonged period
Food processors	When evaluating financial benefits, clearly state assumptions Assign a project manager, however small the investment

Sixty-four per cent are personally involved in such meetings with these other organisations where the outside managers are project managers (23%), finance managers (21%), business development managers (19%) and operations managers (19%) in these other organisations. The use of these meetings with external stakeholders therefore appears to be commonplace for a number of reasons. Table 4.6 shows that external finance advisers and lawyers are more likely to be consulted in business acquisitions, and suppliers in new site/technology projects, which seems sensible.

Question 16 asked about the purpose of the meetings, with yes/no answers. Eight per cent thought their meetings attempted to 'gather views from constituencies or stakeholders', 92% use these meetings to 'evaluate the risk involved in the project', 84% to 'identify key success factors' and over 90% to reach a conclusion on the desirability of the project. This suggests external stakeholders potentially influence the early stages of the psychological and group process (stages 2 to 5) although this conjecture requires further exploration.

Question 17 reveals that in keeping with the traditional management accountants' role, 53 respondents presented information for the SIDs they are involved in, with

Table 4.6 External parties consulted in different project types

Project type (Q9) External parties Q14	New product/ market development	New site/ technology	Acquisitions	Total	Chi-squared*
Suppliers	6	14	2	22	7.34
Customers	6	4	2	12	1.15
Financial advisers/ lawyers	3	5	18	26	13.39
Consultants	4	11	9	24	0.91
Others	8	9	7	24	0.94
Total count	27	43	38	108	23.73
Total %	25	40	35	100	

**Critical values per row (d.f. = 2) at 5% = 5.99 and overall (d.f. = 8) at 5% = 15.51.*
Note: There is a warning that 5 out of 15 cells have values under 5, but results are very significant.

14 involved in evaluation of data and 5 specifically with the evaluation of risk. This seems consistent with involvement through stages 3 to 7. However, a minority (13) reported that they challenged assumptions (consistent with stages 2, 4 and 6) or played 'devil's advocate' in meetings (6 respondents, consistent with stage 5). At least 13 respondents are involved in promoting a project in SID meetings (stage 8), which may indicate that management accountants are becoming more fully involved in building and arguing a business case, especially as 40% now have more general management roles (Table 4.1). In terms of level of seniority, the presenting and promoting roles were fairly evenly split, whereas more senior managers were more likely to challenge assumptions, play devil's advocate or actively participate in project authorisation.

Psychological and group processes

Table 4.7 presents a summary of responses for each of our three psychological themes. It shows a high level of support for the presence of certain psychological attributes, with 69% using brainstorming techniques and 67% using mental pictures of the SID. Less significant, but still notable is the 52% who report drawing on intuition (gut feelings, hunches or flashes of ideas).

Eighty-one per cent make comparisons with previous experience and 66% use these as base values or tolerance ranges, which exemplify anchoring and adjustment. Notable sources of information accessed for specific projects are information on customers (86%), financial projections and business risk factors (both 95%), and supply chain information (78%), but less information was available on shareholders' views (32%). Seventy-nine per cent found the pace of decision-making problematic and 69% were influenced by updated financial projections, the recency of which changed their views on the project.

There is interesting evidence of political behaviour within organisations. For example, 57% witness temporary alliances forming to a significant extent and 69% report 'corridor' meetings or the equivalent as well the views of superior managers being influential (82%). In apparent contrast, there is a high level of use of formal systems, including decision support software.

In exploring these responses further, the mean scores on our 5-point scale for the psychological questions show at least 12 factors where the mean is above 3 (which generally equates to an OLS of at least 68%), indicating widespread evidence of the behavioural themes we investigated in this survey. Results were analysed further for each type of SID (question 9), to examine whether heuristics were more common in certain project types. The analysis in Table 4.8 shows that mental pictures are most common in new product or new market development projects, and that brainstorming is more common in new product development and new technology projects.

Twelve respondents (13%) gave other examples of group behaviour, including potentially negative behaviours:

- *'isolation of dissenters or blockers for blocking sake'*
- *'personal choice can influence rather than logic or profit projection'*
- *'personal preferences'*
- *'some individuals were more concerned with maintaining local status quo than making the right group decision'*
- *'degree of being parochial'*

Other examples were more potentially positive:

- *'singular focus and huge teamwork'*
- *'scoring system'*
- *'competition from other internal groups with their own SID'*
- *'internal processes ensure expectations are managed'*

Factors which respondents thought were important in gaining consensus were:

- managers who speak their minds forthrightly (88%)
- managers with very different skills (78%)

Table 4.7 Psychological and group processes

	Mean	Standard deviation	Overall support (%)
Heuristics (using mental models and intuition)			
Gut feel, hunches or flashes of ideas (Q18)	2.44	1.21	52
Use of mental pictures of the SID	2.96	1.32	67
Use of brainstorming methods	3.06	1.36	69
Use of industry rules of thumb	2.60	1.35	59
Make comparisons with previous projects (Q19)	3.49	1.35	81
Use base value from previous project and tolerance ranges	2.90	1.28	66
Use of industry benchmarks to evaluate SID	2.85	1.49	63
Use of intuition in risk assessment (Q28)	2.68	1.27	55
Framing (sources of and responses to information)			
Market research (Q23)	3.29	1.49	76
Information on customers	3.52	1.30	86
Supply chain information	3.25	1.55	78
Information on shareholders' views	1.79	1.60	32

Financial projections	4.21	1.10	95
Business risk factors	4.04	0.94	95
Impact of up-to-date financial projections (Q21 = Y/N)	–	–	69
Pace at which SID should proceed was problematic (Q22)	3.17	1.23	79
Consensus (group and socio-political processes)			
Use of informal meetings (Q24 = Y/N)	–	–	88
Use of corridor meetings and internal lobbying	–	–	69
Views of company's top management changed own view (Q25)	3.49	1.21	82
People formed temporary alliances or sub-groups (Q26)	2.67	1.51	57
Disagreement was evident during the SID process	2.66	1.23	57
Agreement was reached after considerable compromise	1.93	1.14	27
Like-minded managers with similar industry experience (Q27)	3.23	1.19	78
Managers with very different skills	3.26	1.26	79
Managers who speak their minds forthrightly	3.57	1.20	88

Table 4.8 Use of heuristics in different project types

Mean scores from Q18 → Project type (Q9) ↓	*n*	Gut feel or hunches	Mental pictures	Brainstorm	Rule of thumb
New product development	13	2.77	3.31	3.31	2.15
New market development	11	2.91	4.00	2.73	2.82
New site or site development	17	2.41	2.65	2.82	2.82
New technology or infrastructure	18	2.06	2.28	3.33	2.06
Acquisitions	23	2.43	2.78	2.78	2.74

- like-minded managers with similar experience in the industry (78%)
- managers with very different experiences (74%)
- managers trained in negotiating skills (64%)

In this category, only 38% thought that 'managers who are socially compatible' were of significant importance in gaining consensus, with a further 25% who thought this important to some extent, making 63%, with the rest (37%) thinking it was either not important at all or simply not applicable. This shows a reasonable support for the 'sociality' argument in personal construct theory that says we may construe in such a way as to understand each other's views.

Summary

This study adds important evidence to earlier surveys on capital budgeting practice (Drury et al., 1993; McIntyre and Coulthurst, 1986; Pike, 1996; Scapens and Sale, 1981; Scholl et al., 1978) to elucidate the process of SID-making. It also suggests that examples of managerial behaviour (drawn from psychology) are common and widespread. However, these are not necessarily substitutes for the use of formal manuals or approval procedures but appear to be complementary and an integrated part of the SID process. The key findings from the survey are summarised in the next chapter.

Chapter 5

Summary of Research Findings and Implications

Summary of main findings

The key findings from this study are:

- There is widespread support for an emerging model of the SID process, involving accountants and other managers in up to 10 stages, of which the application of project appraisal techniques is just one.
- There are two additional stages, not previously recognised in the SID literature – an implementation and testing phase before the post-audit stage – and a change management phase to sustain and embed the benefits of the project, especially in business acquisitions.
- Companies tend to require standard SID procedures, with assumptions stated and top management approval, but few require dissenting opinions to be reported.
- Most companies (90%) now use spreadsheet models to support SID-making, and half use critical path analysis (project management software). Whilst few use specialist decision aid software, only 6% use no decision support software at all.

- 37 respondents (41%) made some suggestions for improvement to the SID process in their company, 1 stated that no improvements were necessary, and the remainder chose not to reply to this free text question. The most common calls are for greater compliance or more rigorous evaluation of opportunities or wider consultation.
- There is an increasing need for managers to consult various parties external to the organisation on whom the success of the project may rely, especially in acquisitions where the quality of external information, e.g. financial and legal is critical, or new site/technology projects where suppliers are consulted.
- There is almost as much evidence of psychological and socio-political processes (heuristics, framing and consensus) involved in strategic decisions as there is for the formal financial projections and project appraisal techniques. Strategic decisions involve cognitive processes as well as formal analytical models.
- There is significant use of brainstorming (especially in new product development or technology projects) and mental pictures (heuristics), especially in new product/market development type projects.
- Influence from market research, customer and supply chain information (framing) is significant, and importance attached to the views of top company management and managers who speak their minds forthrightly. In contrast, there is similar importance attached to like-minded managers with similar industry experience as there is to managers with very different skills. There is little evidence of status quo bias among our respondents, as half reported changing their views as a result of receiving more up-to-date information in question 21, and over 80% reported factors altering their opinions (question 25).
- Business risk factors are as important in the framing of projects as the financial projections (both had 95% support). Prior to Collier et al. (2007) most studies, either found little evidence of formal risk analysis or ignored the issue.

This survey of practising management accountants with first-hand experience of SID-making in senior job roles offers some insights to modern-day business thinking. Interpretation of the findings from this relatively small sample must be made with caution, as it is insufficient to draw firm conclusions for all companies. At one pole, companies may use spreadsheet models, project management software and superior manager intervention to manage the SID process. At the other extreme, managers may use intuition and experience to assert preferences and exert influence at different stages through the process. Due to the number of stages in the SID process, the overriding impression is that both formal and psychological judgements are exercised. To summarise from this study, we conclude that managerial judgement plays an important role in SIDs. Figure 5.1 shows an adapted model of the SID process that suggests how managerial judgement may influence the SID process.

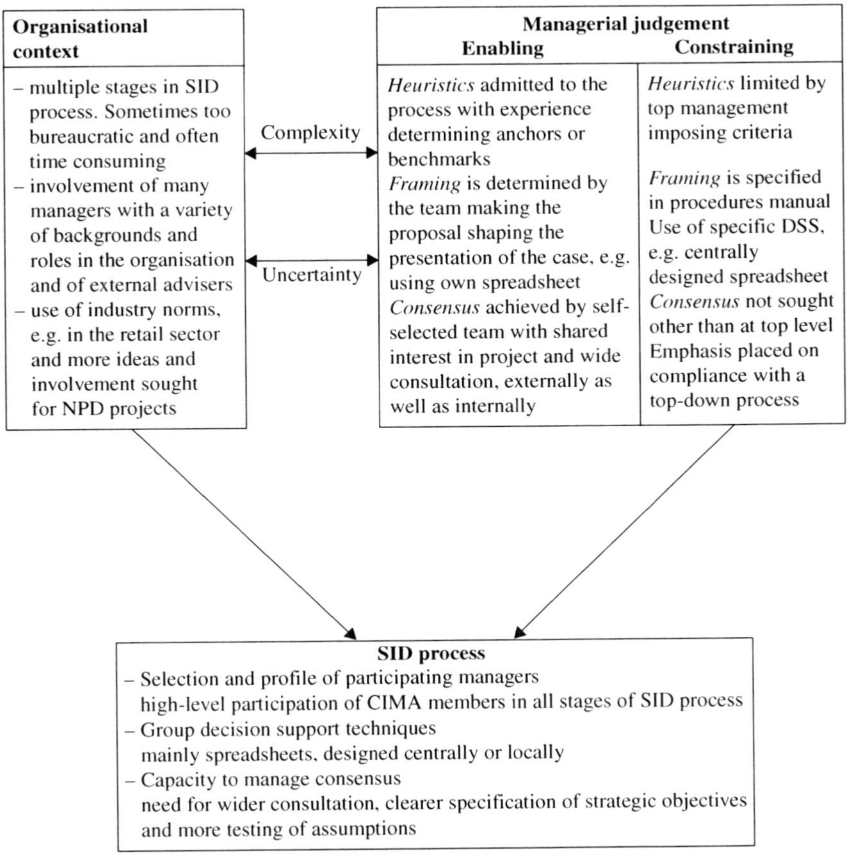

Figure 5.1 Descriptive model of the SID process

This model gives a more complete view of the SID process. The potential for psychological phenomenon to enable or constrain managerial judgement may depend on the management structure and style in the organisation. The extent to which managerial judgement influences the SID process is generally high, but varies across our sample, depending on the level of bureaucracy and top-down procedures. The enabling scenario is consistent with budget delegation to subsidiaries or divisions, but senior managers may feel that more compliance with corporate procedures is desirable. The constraining scenario is consistent with a centrally determined process, where some managers feel there is more scope for 'gut feel' or intuition. 'This model cannot yet be described as definitive, but Appendix 4 shows how it applies to six case organisations. This shows how the model may usefully guide further research.'

Implications for management accounting literature

Whilst some of the findings may not be new to experienced management accountants and practitioners, there is little recognition of the pre-evaluation and post-evaluation stages in the SID process, or the psychological behaviour involved in the decision process in management accounting literature. Since this study was undertaken some 'decision-maker effects' have been covered in a management accounting literature review, but this is limited to agency theory-based research and experimental psychology-based research (Haka, 2007, pp. 708–715).

However, most management accounting textbooks covering capital investment appraisal techniques need to do more to acknowledge the context in which SIDs take place, and the human behaviour, both individual and group, which help to depict the complex reality in which these decisions are made. The model above should provide a more complete picture of the SID process to inform both teaching and further research.

The whole issue of whether and when the group board and the project team interact in the SID process, especially at the crucial stages in decision-making, is a vital area for future research.

Implications for management accountants

For many experienced management accountants, such as our participants in the survey, the complexity of the SIDs reported here will come as no surprise, although the variety of stages and management practices may offer insights. Previous research has not reported such widespread use of intuitive and qualitative methods in SIDs. In contrast with experimental research, this survey reveals the psychological concepts of heuristics, framing and cognitive group processes having a pervasive influence across industry sectors and types of project.

The findings have implications for management accountants, especially those with limited experience or involvement in SIDs in organisations, where knowledge of the human behavioural aspects of SIDs can prepare them for the realities of SIDs. Indeed, Hillson and Murray-Webster (2005, pp. 146–152) emphasise the need for managers to be self-aware of risk attitudes and heuristics in order to achieve high-quality decision-making and effective risk management. They claim that emotional intelligence testing and training is essential for decision-takers. Whilst this recommendation is what one might expect from authors offering such training and consultancy services, there is certainly merit in advocating self-awareness and decision-making skills, beyond the analytical techniques that may be tested in CIMA membership examinations.

Due to the seniority in their organisations and the broad managerial roles undertaken by CIMA members in our survey, the implications set out below for the management of organisations are equally important for CIMA members, especially the suggestions for improvements to the SID process.

Implications for management of organisations

It is suggested that this publication may assist organisations in benchmarking their own SID practice. The full survey questionnaire and results have been included in Appendices 1 and 2 to enable others to use all or part of the same instrument in internal diagnostics. If all members of a project team or a senior management group or committee were to answer the same questions, the results could be compared to those from the cross-sectional survey to reveal whether practice in the organisation is below or above average.

From an organisational learning perspective, a training needs analysis could be undertaken on decision-making skills, covering awareness of decision-taker behaviours and risk attitudes, and other areas highlighted by respondents as areas for improvement in their organisations. Professional accountancy curricula cover the analytical skills that are needed for effective decision-making, but cannot provide for some of the softer skills, such as negotiation, gaining consensus and information sharing potentially relevant to effective SID-making. There are CPD training solutions offered by CIMA and by many commercial organisations that can help financial and non-financial managers develop a range of 'softer' skills which can include awareness of psychological phenomena but which need to be applied in specific organisational contexts.

There were two key findings that might sound a warning to those responsible for approving SIDs in their organisation – usually the group board. Fifty-seven per cent reported that 'disagreement was evident during the SID process' to a great, considerable or reasonable extent (question 26), but only 52% reported that 'dissenting opinions are required to be reported in their company'. When combined this means the group board might never know of any dissent. Whether the newly identified stages (implementation and testing, and change management) address this issue and attempt to mitigate it is unknown. In the authors' experience, the post-decision stages of project management tend to involve different teams of managers and issues, especially reasons for dissenting views, raised during pre-decision meetings are rarely conveyed to implementation teams. Good practice at these later stages needs to be explored.

Whilst only three respondents called for improvement in post-completion reviews, this appears on the surface to be contradictory. The fact that only 74% report post-completion reviews taking place in their company (question 10) is interesting in this respect. Therefore there are still firms not conducting such reviews at all. Together these issues suggest learning to understand how the effective SID is chosen is possibly haphazard, firm or manager specific. This compares with 72% in UK firms in 1992

(Pike, 1996) and Myers (1991) finding in US companies, where although 76% of firms conducted post-audit evaluations, only 33% were perceived as being conducted properly. The most commonly reported areas for improvement (Table 5.1) can be used as a checklist for organisations when reviewing SIDs and capital budgeting procedures manuals.

Table 5.1 Suggestions to improve SID-making process

Suggestions for improvement (*n* = 59)	Count (%)
Compliance with, more trust in and commitment to process	10 (17%)
Timing issues – more speed, faster roll-outs and less time on operational issues	10 (17%)
Improvement in post-completion reviews	3 (5%)
Better change management	2 (3%)
Total for process issues	25 (42%)
Consensus and communication issues – including wider consultation, clearer definition of strategic objectives, review of assumptions and more feedback to stakeholders	15 (26%)
Framing – more rigorous evaluation of opportunities, benefits, success and risks, and more sensitivity analysis	14 (24%)
More use of gut feel and intuition and less bureaucracy or formality	5 (8%)
Total for psychological issues	34 (58%)

Implications for stakeholders

Investors seek to rely on management of organisations to ensure they make sound strategic decisions. They should appreciate how human behaviour might influence decisions and how managerial judgement might be exercised. The issues of consultation, communication and transparency in terms of procedures adopted for SIDs and project risk assessment and management will be vital in achieving good investor relations. Direct investor involvement is only significant in acquisition type projects, so there may be more scope for consultation on other projects.

There has been clearer reporting of risk management practices since the Combined Code on Corporate Governance (2003) was issued by the Financial Reporting

Council. Our survey showed that 53% use intuitive risk assessment methods, which is not necessarily inappropriate, especially as 77% also report use of probabilistic methods, but stakeholders may not appreciate the scope for heuristics and bias in the risk assessment of projects and how this can impact on the outcome of SIDs. Intuitive methods are not inherently bad, as some writers on heuristics and bias may imply, but they need to be used wisely by experienced practitioners and balanced with other more analytical methods, and a more formal learning from past decisions seems a sound place to begin.

For stakeholders such as customers, suppliers, external advisers and consultants, the implication of both the existing level of external consultation and the perceived need for more consultation noted above will be the need for more inter-firm meetings and communications. Any consultation process may be time-consuming, but might well be desirable for all parties concerned, especially if awareness of the behavioural aspects of SID-making is raised.

We have confirmed that managerial judgement and the range of group behaviours managers engage in are important in SIDs. It would be useful in future research on SID-making to explore further how this impacts at different stages and how firm performance is affected.

References

Bazerman, M.H., 2006. Judgement in Managerial Decision Making, sixth ed. New York, John Wiley.

Bower, J.L., 1986. Managing the Resource Allocation Process. Harvard Business School Press, Boston, MA.

Claxton, G., 1998. Knowing without knowing why. Psychologist 11 (5), 217–220.

Collier, P., Berry, A.J., Burke, G.T., 2007. Risk and Management Accounting: Best Practice Guidelines for Enterprise-Wide Internal Control Procedures. Elsevier, Oxford.

Dawes, R.M., Kragt, A.J.C.v.d., Orbell, J.M., 1988. Not me or thee but we: The importance of group identity in eliciting cooperation in dilemma situations: experimental manipulations. Acta Psychol. 68, 83–97.

Drury, C., Braund, S., Osborne, P., Tayles, M., 1993. A Survey of Management Accounting Practices in UK Manufacturing Companies. The Chartered Association of Certified Accountants, Glasgow.

Dyson, R.G., 1990. Strategic Planning: Models and Analytical Techniques. John Wiley & Sons, Chichester.

Eden, C., Simpson, P., 1989. SODA and cognitive mapping in practice. In: Rosenhead, J. (Ed.), Rational Analysis for a Problematic World. John Wiley, Chichester, pp. 43–70.

Eisenhardt, K.M., 1989. Making fast strategic decisions in high-velocity environments. Acad. Manag. J. 32 (3), 543–576.

Epley, N., Gilovich, T., 2002. Putting adjustment back in the anchoring and adjustment heuristic. In: Gilovich, T., Griffin, D., Kahneman, D. (Eds.) Heuristics and Biases. Cambridge University Press, New York, pp. 139–149.

Emery, M., 2002. Power Hunch: Living an Intuitive Life. Beyond Words Publishing, Hillsboro, OR.

Gilovich, T., Griffin, D., Kahneman, D., 2002. Heuristics and Biases. Cambridge University Press, New York.

Haka, S., 2007. A review of the literature on capital budgeting and investment appraisal: past, present, and future musings. In: Chapman, C.S., Hopwood, A.G., Shields, M.D. (Eds.) Handbook of Management Accounting Research, vol. 2. Elsevier, Oxford, p. 697–728.

Hall, J., 1971. Decisions, decisions, decisions. Psychol. Today November, 51–54, 86–88.

Handy, C., 1993. Understanding Organizations, fourth ed. Penguin, London.

Harris, E.P., 1999. Project risk assessment: a European field study. Br. Account. Rev. 31 (3), 347–371.

Hastie, R., Dawes, R., 2001. Rational Choice in an Uncertain World. Sage, Thousand Oaks.

Haynes, W.W., Solomon, M.B., 1962. A misplaced emphasis in capital budgeting. Q. Rev. Econ. Bus. February, 39–46.

Hickson, D.J., Butler, R.J., Cray, D., Mallory, G.R., Wilson, D.C., 1986. Top Decisions: Strategic Decision-Making in Organizations. Jossey-Bass, San Francisco, CA.

Hillson, D., Murray-Webster, R., 2005. Understanding and Managing Risk Attitude. Gower, Aldershot.

Hodgkinson, G.P., Brown, N.J., et al., 1999. Breaking the frame: an analysis of strategic cognition and decision making under uncertainty. Strateg. Manag. J. 20, 977–985.

Holloman, C.R., 1992. Using both head and heart in managerial decision making. Ind. Manag. 34 (6), 7–10.

Huff, A.S., Jenkins, M. (Eds.), 2002. Mapping Strategic Knowledge. Sage, London.

Janis, I.L., 1982. Groupthink: Psychological Studies of Policy Decisions and Fiascoes, second ed. Houghton Mifflin, Boston, MA.

Jones, T.C., Dugdale, D., 1994. Academic and practitioner rationality: the case of investment appraisal. Br. Account. Rev. 26 (1), 3–25.

Kahneman, D., Frederick, S., 2002. Representativeness revisited: attribute substitution in intuitive judgement. In: Gilovich, T., Griffin, D., Kahneman, D. (Eds.) Heuristics and Biases. Cambridge University Press, New York, pp. 49–81.

Kahneman, D., Tversky, A., 1982. On the study of statistical intuitions. Cognition 11, 123–141.

Kelly, G.A., 1955. The Psychology of Personal Constructs: A Theory of Personality. Norton, New York.

King, P., 1975. Is the emphasis of capital budgeting theory misplaced? J. Bus. Fin. Accoun. 2 (1), 69–82.

Lumijärvi, O.P., 1991. Selling of capital investments to top management. Manag. Account. Res. 2 (2), 171–188.

Mangione, T.W., 1995. Mail Surveys: Improving the Quality. Sage, Thousand Oaks, CA.

McIntyre, A.D., Coulthurst, N.J., 1986. Capital Budgeting Practices in Medium-Sized Businesses – A Survey. CIMA, London.

Mintzberg, H.D., Raisinghani, D., Théorêt, A., 1976. The structure of unstructured decision processes. Adm. Sci. Q. 21 (2), 246–275.

Mohammed, S., 2001. Toward an understanding of cognitive consensus in a group decision-making context. J. Appl. Behav. Sci. 37 (4), 408–425.

Myers, M.D., Gordon, L., Hamer, M., 1991. Postauditing capital assets and firm performance: an empirical investigation. Manag. Decis. Econ. 12, 317–327.

Pettigrew, A.M., 1973. The Politics of Organizational Decision-Making. Tavistock, London.

Pike, R.H., 1996. A longitudinal survey on capital budgeting practices. J. Bus. Fin. Accoun, 23 (1), 79–92.

Pike, R., Neale, B., 1996. Corporate Finance and Investment: Decisions and Strategies, second ed. Prentice Hall, Hemel Hempstead, Herts.
Salton, G.J., 2000. Getting a grip on group behaviour. Ind. Manag. 42 (6), 26–33.
Samuelson, W., Zeckhauser, R., 1988. Status quo bias in decision making. J. Risk Uncertain. (I), 7–59.
Scapens, R.W., Sale, J.T., 1981. Performance measurement and formal capital expenditure controls in divisionalised companies. J. Bus. Fin. Account. (Autumn), 389–420.
Scholl, L.D., Sundem, G.L., Geijsbeek, W.R., 1978. Survey and analysis of capital budgeting methods. J. Fin. 33 (1), 281–287.
Schweiger, D.M., Sandberg, W.R., Ragan, J.W., 1986. Group approaches for improving strategic decision making: a comparative analysis of dialectical inquiry, devil's advocacy, and consensus. Acad. Manag. J. 29 (1), 51–71.
Schwenk, C.R., 1988. The cognitive perspective on strategic decision making. J. Manag. Stud. 25 (1), 41–55.
Simon, H.A., 1957. Models of Man. John Wiley & Sons, Inc, New York.
Simon, H.A., 1976. Administrative Behaviour: A Study of Decision Making in Administrative Organisations. Free Press, Collier Macmillan, New York.
Slovic, P., Fischhoff, B., et al., 1977. Behavioural decision theory. Ann. Rev. Psychol. 28, 1–39.
Staw, B.M., 1981. The escalation of commitment to a course of action. Acad. Manag. Rev. 6, 577–587.
Tse, A.C.B., 1998. Comparing the response rate, response speed and response quality of two methods of sending questionnaires: e-mail vs. mail. J. Mark. Res. Soc. 40 (4), 353–361.
Tversky, A., Kahneman, D., 1971. Belief in the law of small numbers. Psychol. Bull. (76), 105–110.
Tversky, A., Kahneman, D., 1974. Judgement under uncertainty: heuristics and biases. Science 185 (September), 1124–1131.
Tversky, A., Kahneman, D., 1986. Rational choice and the framing of decisions. J. Bus. 59 (4), S251–S278.
Tversky, A., Kahneman, D., 1991. Loss aversion in riskless choice: a reference-dependent model. Q. J. Econ. 106, 1039–1061.

Appendix 1: Questionnaire

Thank you for agreeing to complete this questionnaire, which should take about 15 minutes of your time. The questionnaire is divided into four sections (A to D). Please complete all the sections.

Section A – Background information

1. **What is the name of your company?**
2. **What is your job title?**
3. **What is your professional background?**
   - ☐ Accounting (Financial)
   - ☐ Accounting (Management)
   - ☐ Engineering
   - ☐ Finance
   - ☐ Information Systems
   - ☐ Legal
   - ☐ Marketing
   - ☐ Others (*please specify*)
4. **How long have you worked for the company?**
   - ☐ 0–5 years
   - ☐ 6–10 years
   - ☐ 11–15 years
   - ☐ 16–20 years
   - ☐ 21+ years
5. **How long have you been in your current position?**
   - ☐ 0–5 years
   - ☐ 6–10 years
   - ☐ 11–15 years
   - ☐ 16–20 years
   - ☐ 21+ years

6. **Had you worked in a similar position in other companies before?**
   - ☐ Yes
   - ☐ No

   If No go to Section B

7. **How long had you worked in a similar position in other companies before joining the current company?**
   - ☐ 0–5 years
   - ☐ 6–10 years
   - ☐ 11–15 years
   - ☐ 16–20 years
   - ☐ 21+ years

Guidance on completing Sections B and C

Please read and answer the following questions with specific strategic investment decision or decisions (SIDs), in which you were involved, in mind.

For the purpose of this research study, we have defined SIDs to include decisions concerning long-term investment in risky capital assets (e.g. the purchase or expansion of equipment or production facilities; or expenditures with direct impact on the company's ability to meet its strategic objectives).

Where explanation is required, please write in as much detail as possible in the space provided. Further guidance is provided after the particular questions concerned.

Section B – Involvement in SIDs

8. **What types of SID have you been involved with?** (*please select all that apply*)
   - ☐ New product development
   - ☐ New market development (new customers/clients)
   - ☐ New site or site development (operating facilities, e.g. new location, relocation, expansion)
   - ☐ New technology or infrastructure, e.g. computer system development/ replacement
   - ☐ Acquisitions of business assets or companies
   - ☐ Compliance (new legislation, e.g. health and safety)
   - ☐ Others (e.g. decommissioning, downsizing, business process design) (*please specify*)

   Please choose the SPECIFIC PROJECT that you will focus on when answering the following questions.

9. **Which type of project will be the focus of your answers?**
   - ☐ New product development
   - ☐ New market development (new customers/clients)
   - ☐ New site or site development (operating facilities, e.g. new location, relocation, expansion)
   - ☐ New technology or infrastructure, e.g. computer system development/ replacement
   - ☐ Acquisitions of business assets or companies
   - ☐ Compliance (new legislation, e.g. health and safety)
   - ☐ Others (e.g. decommissioning, downsizing, business process design) (*please specify*)

10. **For the specific project you have in mind, which of the following stages applies in your company and which were you personally involved in?** (*please select all that apply*)

	Does it apply in your company?	Were you involved?
Scanning for project opportunities		
Defining possible projects and formulating alternatives or strategic options		
Generation of project data		
Making preliminary assumptions; shaping project outline		
Early screening discussion on project idea to decide if it should be pursued		
Estimation of cash flow/financial data		
Formal evaluation of the project: using project appraisal techniques, e.g. discounted cash flow (DCF)		
Progression through the company; persuading senior managers to support the project		
Authorisation of the project		
Post-audit evaluation (project review)		
Other stages (*please specify*)		

11. **Did your involvement require formal* meetings with other managers within your company? (*for the purposes of this questionnaire, 'formal' is defined as planned, of a formally recognised group, e.g. divisional board, formal committee, routine project team or advisory group)**
   - ☐ Yes
   - ☐ No

   If No, go to question 13

12. **Please give the job titles of all the internal managers involved in the formal meetings** (*please select all that apply or the nearest equivalent*).
   - ☐ Business development manager
   - ☐ Finance manager/management accountant
   - ☐ Marketing manager
   - ☐ IT manager
   - ☐ Operations manager
   - ☐ Project manager
   - ☐ Production manager
   - ☐ Others (*please specify*)

13. **Did your involvement require formal meetings with other managers outside your company?**
   - ☐ Yes
   - ☐ No

   If No, go to question 16

14. **What did the external managers represent in terms of the specific project?** (*please select all that apply*)
   - ☐ Supplier organisations
   - ☐ Customer organisations
   - ☐ Financing organisations
   - ☐ Consultants
   - ☐ Government departments
   - ☐ Others (*please specify*)

15. **Please give the job titles of the external managers involved in the formal meetings** (*please select all that apply*)
   - ☐ Business development manager
   - ☐ Finance manager
   - ☐ Marketing manager
   - ☐ IT manager
   - ☐ Operations manager
   - ☐ Project manager
   - ☐ Production manager
   - ☐ Others (*please specify*)

16. **In your opinion did the meetings attempt to:**

	Yes	No
Gather views from various constituencies or stakeholders?		
Evaluate the risk involved in the project?		
Handle any complexity by constructing a model?		
Identify key success factors?		
Attach probabilities to alternative outcomes?		
Reach consensus amongst the various participants or constituencies on relevant issues?		
Reach a decision on the desirability of the project?		
Reach a conclusion on the issues being discussed?		
Resolve other issue(s)? Please specify		

17. **Please give a brief description of your involvement in the meeting(s). What role did you play in the proceeding(s), e.g. presenting information, promoting the project, active or passive role, devil's advocate, etc?**

From question 18 onwards, where you are asked to rank your chosen option, the scales 5 to 1 mean the following: 5 = to a great extent; 4 = considerable extent; 3 = reasonable extent; 2 = some extent and 1 = hardly at all.

18. **To what extent did you use the following during the SID?** (*please rank on a scale of 5 – to a great extent to 1 – hardly at all*)

	To a great extent				Hardly at all	Not applicable
	5	4	3	2	1	
Gut feeling or hunches or flashes of ideas						
Mental pictures of the SID in your mind						
Brainstorming						
Industry's rule of thumb						
Others (*please specify*)						

19. **To what extent were the following important during the SID?** (*please rank on a scale of 5 – to a great extent to 1 – hardly at all*)

	To a great extent				Hardly at all	Not applicable
	5	4	3	2	1	
Comparing and contrasting new project opportunities with similar projects you were previously involved with						
Use of stereotypes to classify projects						
Use of base value from previous projects and tolerance ranges						
Use of industry benchmark to evaluate the SID						
Use of other benchmarks to evaluate the SID (*please specify*)						

Section C – Influences on SIDs

20. **Recollecting your involvement in the decision-making process, to what extent was each of the following aspects of your personal knowledge and experience important in influencing the SID?** (*please rank on a scale of 5 – to a great extent to 1 – hardly at all*)

	To a great extent				Hardly at all	Not applicable
	5	4	3	2	1	
Technical experience						
Managerial experience						
Knowledge of competitors						
Your professional background						
Knowledge of inner workings/ processes within your company						

(*Continued*)

	To a great extent				Hardly at all	Not applicable
Knowledge of strategy formulation in your company						
Knowledge and experience of other managers involved in the SID process						
Others (*please specify*)						

21. **Did your views of the project change as a result of receiving more up-to-date (real-time) information about the following?**

	Yes	No
Change in the definition of the project		
Technological issues		
Logistical issues		
The impact of financial projections		
The need to act quickly to meet datelines		
Other information (*please specify*)		

22. **To what extent were the following aspects of the SID considered problematic?** (*please rank on a scale of 5 – to a great extent to 1 – hardly at all*)

	To a great extent				Hardly at all	Not applicable
	5	4	3	2	1	
Specific objectives of the SID						
Overall strategic objectives of the organisation						
Procedures for evaluating the SID						

(*Continued*)

	To a great extent				Hardly at all	Not applicable
Personal agendas						
The pace at which matters should proceed						
Issues of professional ethics and responsibility						
The track record of the proposer of the SID						
Others (*please specify*)						

23. **To what extent did you have access to the following information for your specific project?** (*Please rank, on a scale of 5 – to a great extent to 1 – hardly at all, the extent to which the information was available.*)

	To a great extent				Hardly at all	Not applicable
	5	4	3	2	1	
Market research (e.g. market size, share, growth, competitors' action, product price changes etc.)						
Information on customers/ users						
Supply chain information						
Suppliers' views						
Views of employees at operational level						
Information on shareholders' views						
Other stakeholders information, e.g. government						
Financial projections						
Business risk factors						
Others (*please specify*)						

24. **Were any of the following used during the SID process?** (*please indicate whether or not the process is applicable in your company and whether or not you were involved in the process*)

	Does it apply in your company?	Were you involved?
Informal (ad hoc rather than routine, planned within shorter notice) meetings		
Corridor (unscheduled) meetings and internal lobbying		
Political lobbying with external agencies, e.g. government department and trade associations		
Using informal opportunities (e.g. at social functions) to influence decision-making		
Other informal process(es): *please specify*		

25. **For the specific project, to what extent did each of the following alter your opinion on the SID?** (*please rank on a scale of 5 – to a great extent to 1 – hardly at all*)

	To a great extent				Hardly at all	Not applicable
	5	4	3	2	1	
Discussion during formal meetings						
Informal discussions and interaction with managers involved in the SID						
Discussions and interaction with other managers not involved in the SID						

(Continued)

	To a great extent				Hardly at all	Not applicable
Views of the company's top management[†]						
Others (*please specify*)						

[†]*For this research study, we have defined 'top management' to include head office management, senior management or group management. As the use of the term may differ from company to company, please keep this in mind when completing this questionnaire.*

26. **To what the extent did the following occur during the SID?** (*please rank on a scale of 5 – to a great extent to 1 – hardly at all*)

	To a great extent				Hardly at all	Not applicable
	5	4	3	2	1	
People formed temporary alliances or subgroups expressly for the purpose of this SID						
Disagreement was evident during the SID process						
The proposer's track record with SIDs influenced the SID						
Agreement was reached after considerable compromise						
Other examples of group behaviour (*please specify*)						

27. **To what extent was each of the following important in gaining a consensus on the SID?** (*please rank on a scale of 5 – to a great extent to 1 – hardly at all*)

	To a great extent				Hardly at all	Not applicable
	5	4	3	2	1	

(*Continued*)

	To a great extent				Hardly at all	Not applicable
Managers who are socially compatible						
Like-minded managers with similar experience in the industry						
Managers with very different experiences						
Managers with very different skills						
Managers who speak their minds forthrightly						
Managers who respect superiors' opinions						
Managers trained in negotiating skills						
Others (*please specify*)						

28. **To what extent was each of the following used to assess the risk(s) associated with the SID(s)?** (*please rank on a scale of 5 – to a great extent to 1 – hardly at all*)

	To a great extent				Hardly at all	Not applicable
	5	4	3	2	1	
Evaluation of expected outcomes (based on probability or likelihood of alternative outcomes)						
Comparison with risk profile of past projects						
Intuition						
Others (*please specify*)						

29. **To what extent does your company require each of the following during SID-making process?** (*please rank on a scale of 5 – to a great extent to 1 – hardly at all*)

	To a great extent 5	4	3	2	Hardly at all 1	Not applicable
A set of standard procedures (e.g. following a procedures manual or standard instructions) to be employed when assessing SIDs						
Assumptions underlying your decision to be stated						
Top management's approval						
Dissenting opinions to be reported						
An individual manager to champion and be responsible for the SID						
Others (*please specify*)						

30. **Which of the following Decision Support Software (DSS) did you use for appraising the SID?**
   - ☐ Spreadsheet Model
   - ☐ Specific Decision Support Package
   - ☐ Decision Trees
   - ☐ Critical Path Analysis
   - ☐ Others (*please specify*)
   - ☐ No DSS was used

Section D – Concluding section

31. **To what extent is the SID-making process for the specific project you had in mind typical in your organisation in terms of the normal procedures used in your organisation?**

To a great extent				Hardly at all
5	4	3	2	1

32. **What suggestions would you offer to improve the SID-making process in your organisation?**

Appendix 2: Summary of Survey Responses

Thank you for agreeing to complete this questionnaire, which should take about 15 minutes of your time. The questionnaire is divided into four sections (A to D). Please complete all the sections.

***n* = 91 VALUES AS PERCENTAGES**

Section A – Background information

1. **What is the name of your company?** **(*n* = 65)** **65 companies**
2. **What is your job title?** **(*n* = 91)**
3. **What is your professional background?** **(*n* = 91)**

☐ Accounting (Financial)	**14.3**
☐ Accounting (Management)	**89.0**
☐ Engineering	**3.3**
☐ Finance	**6.6**
☐ Information Systems	**3.3**
☐ Legal	**0**
☐ Marketing	**0**
☐ Other (*please specify*)	**1.1**

4. **How long have you worked for the company?** **(*n* = 91)**

☐ 0–5 years	**25.3**
☐ 6–10 years	**23.1**
☐ 11–15 years	**18.7**
☐ 16–20 years	**15.4**
☐ 21 + years	**17.5**

5. **How long have you been in your current position?** **(*n* = 91)**

☐ 0–5 years	**81.3**
☐ 6–10 years	**13.2**
☐ 11–15 years	**3.3**

☐ 16–20 years 1.1
☐ 21 + years 1.1

6. **Had you worked in a similar position in other companies before?** (*n* = 91)
☐ Yes 39.6
☐ No 60.4
If No, go to Section B

7. **How long had you worked in a similar position in other companies before joining the current company?** (*n* = 36)
☐ 0–5 years 52.8
☐ 6–10 years 25.0
☐ 11–15 years 16.7
☐ 16–20 years 2.8
☐ 21 + years 2.8

Guidance on completing Sections B and C

Please read and answer the following questions with specific strategic investment decision or decisions (SIDs), in which you were involved, in mind.

For the purpose of this research study, we have defined SIDs to include decisions concerning long-term investment in risky capital assets (e.g. the purchase or expansion of equipment or production facilities; or expenditures with direct impact on the company's ability to meet its strategic objectives).

Where explanation is required, please write in as much detail as possible in the space provided. Further guidance is provided after the particular questions concerned.

Section B – Involvement in SIDs

8. **What types of SID have you been involved with?** (*please select all that apply*) (*n* = 91)

	Rank	
☐ New product development	4	47.3
☐ New market development (new customers/clients)	6	41.8
☐ New site or site development (operating facilities, e.g. new location, relocation, expansion)	2	68.1
☐ New technology or infrastructure, e.g. computer system development/replacement	1	70.3
☐ Acquisitions of business assets or companies	3	60.4
☐ Compliance (new legislation, e.g. health and safety)	7	34.1

☐ Other (e.g. decommissioning, downsizing, business process design) (*please specify*) **5** **46.2**

***Please choose the* SPECIFIC PROJECT *that you will focus on when answering the following questions*.**

9. **Which type of project will be the focus of your answers?** **($n = 91$)**
   - ☐ New product development **14.3**
   - ☐ New market development (new customers/clients) **11.0**
   - ☐ New site or site development (operating facilities, e.g. new location, relocation, expansion) **20.9**
   - ☐ New technology or infrastructure, e.g. computer system development/replacement **17.6**
   - ☐ Acquisitions of business assets or companies **26.4**
   - ☐ Compliance (new legislation, e.g. health and safety) **1.1**
   - ☐ Other (e.g. decommissioning, downsizing, business process design) (*please specify*) **8.7**

10. **For the specific project you have in mind, which of the following stages applies in your company and which were you personally involved in?** (*please select all that apply*) **($n = 91$)**

	Does it apply in your company?	Were you involved?
Scanning for project opportunities	**75.8**	**38.5**
Defining possible projects and formulating alternatives or strategic options	**89.0**	**61.5**
Generation of project data	**82.4**	**58.2**
Making preliminary assumptions; shaping project outline	**92.3**	**62.6**
Early screening discussion on project idea to decide if it should be pursued	**86.8**	**65.9**
Estimation of cash flow/ financial data	**97.8**	**75.8**

(*Continued*)

		Does it apply in your company?	Were you involved?
Formal evaluation of the project: using project appraisal techniques, e.g. Discounted Cash Flow (DCF)		**82.4**	**65.9**
Progression through the company; persuading senior managers to support the project		**91.2**	**73.6**
Authorisation of the project		**91.2**	**53.8**
Post-audit evaluation (project review)		**73.6**	**48.4**
Other stages (*please specify*)	**(n = 15, 76 missing)**	**100.0**	**80.0**

11. **Did your involvement require formal* meetings with other managers within your company? (*for the purposes of this questionnaire, 'formal' is defined as planned, of a formally recognised group, e.g. divisional board, formal committee, routine project team or advisory group)** **(n = 91)**
    - ☐ Yes **97.8**
    - ☐ No **2.2**

    If No, go to question 13

12. **Please give the job titles of all the internal managers involved in the formal meetings** (*please select all that apply or the nearest equivalent*). **(n = 90)**
    - ☐ Business development manager **48.9**
    - ☐ Finance manager/management accountant **81.1**
    - ☐ Marketing manager **28.9**
    - ☐ IT manager **40.0**
    - ☐ Operations manager **58.9**
    - ☐ Project manager **61.1**
    - ☐ Production manager **27.8**
    - ☐ Others (*please specify*) **48.9**

13. **Did your involvement require formal meetings with other managers outside your company?** **(n = 91)**
    - ☐ Yes **63.7**
    - ☐ No (*If No, go to question 16*) **36.3**

14. **What did the external managers represent in terms of the specific project?** (*please select all that apply*) (*n* = 58)

☐ Supplier organisations	30.0
☐ Customer organisations	16.3
☐ Financing organisations	16.3
☐ Consultants	38.8
☐ Government departments	15.0
☐ Others (*please specify*)	22.8

15. **Please give the job titles of the external managers involved in the formal meetings** (*please select all that apply*). (*n* = 58)

☐ Business development manager	18.8
☐ Finance manager	21.3
☐ Marketing manager	10.0
☐ IT manager	10.0
☐ Operations manager	18.8
☐ Project manager	22.5
☐ Production manager	6.3
☐ Others (*please specify*)	33.8

16. **In your opinion did the meetings attempt to:** (*n* = 91)

	Yes	No
Gather views from various constituencies or stakeholders?	79.8	20.2
Evaluate the risk involved in the project?	92.3	7.7
Handle any complexity by constructing a model?	52.8	47.2
Identify key success factors?	84.4	15.6
Attach probabilities to alternative outcomes?	48.9	51.1
Reach consensus amongst the various participants or constituencies on relevant issues?	86.5	13.5
Reach a decision on the desirability of the project?	88.8	11.2
Reach a conclusion on the issues being discussed?	92.0	8.0
Resolve other issue(s)? *Please specify.*	100.0	0

17. **Please give a brief description of your involvement in the meeting(s). What role did you play in the proceeding(s), e.g. presenting information, promoting the project, active or passive role, devil's advocate, etc?** (*n* = 82)

KEY THEMES THAT HAVE EMERGED

Presenting information	(48 times)	**Evaluation of data**	(14 times)
Challenging project assumptions	(13 times)	**Promoting project**	(12 times)

Devil's advocate (5 times) Risk evaluation (5 times)

From question 18 onwards, where you are asked to rank your chosen option, the scales 5 to 1 mean the following: 5 = to a great extent; 4 = considerable extent; 3 = reasonable extent; 2 = some extent and 1 = hardly at all.

18. **To what extent did you use the following during the SID?** (*please rank on a scale of 5 – to a great extent to 1 – hardly at all*) **(*n* = 91)**

(OLS = overall level of support)

	To a great extent					Hardly at all	Not applicable
	5	4	3	OLS	2	1	
Gut feeling or hunches or flashes of ideas	3.3	16.5	31.9	51.7	20.9	24.2	3.2
Mental pictures of the SID in your mind	7.8	34.4	24.4	66.6	17.8	10.0	5.6
Brainstorming	10.0	37.8	21.1	68.9	15.6	10.0	5.5
Industry's rule of thumb	6.7	18.9	33.3	58.9	17.8	15.5	7.8
Others (*please specify n = 15*)	9.9	6.6	0	16.5	0	0	0

19. **To what extent were the following important during the SID?** (*please rank on a scale of 5 – to a great extent to 1 – hardly at all*) **(*n* = 91)**

	To a great extent					Hardly at all	Not applicable
	5	4	3	OLS	2	1	
Comparing and contrasting new project opportunities with similar projects you were previously involved with	22.0	40.7	18.7	81.4	5.5	9.9	3.2

(*Continued*)

	To a great extent					Hardly at all	Not applicable
Use of stereotypes to classify projects	**3.4**	**10.3**	**18.4**	**32.1**	**23.0**	**35.6**	**9.3**
Use of base value from previous projects and tolerance ranges	**8.9**	**26.7**	**30.0**	**65.6**	**17.8**	**13.3**	**3.3**
Use of industry benchmark to evaluate the SID	**13.8**	**24.1**	**25.3**	**63.2**	**14.9**	**13.8**	**8.1**
Use of other benchmarks to evaluate the SID (*please specify* $n = 36$)	**12.1**	**8.8**	**3.3**	**24.2**	**2.2**	**9.9**	**3.3**

Section C – Influences on SIDs

20. **Recollecting your involvement in the decision-making process, to what extent was each of the following aspects of your personal knowledge and experience important in influencing the SID?** (*please rank on a scale of 5 – to a great extent* to *1 – hardly at all*) **(*n* = 91)**

	To a great extent					Hardly at all	Not applicable
	5	**4**	**3**	**OLS**	**2**	**1**	
Technical experience	**16.7**	**38.9**	**20.0**	**75.6**	**14.4**	**6.7**	**3.3**
Managerial experience	**23.3**	**50.0**	**15.6**	**88.9**	**2.2**	**6.7**	**2.2**
Knowledge of competitors	**13.5**	**27.0**	**21.3**	**61.8**	**16.9**	**16.9**	**4.4**

(*Continued*)

	To a great extent					Hardly at all	Not applicable
Your professional background	**26.7**	**50.0**	**20.0**	**96.7**	**2.2**	**0**	**1.1**
Knowledge of inner workings/ processes within your company	**36.7**	**43.3**	**17.8**	**97.8**	**1.1**	**0**	**1.1**
Knowledge of strategy formulation in your company	**22.2**	**47.8**	**22.2**	**92.2**	**5.6**	**1.1**	**1.1**
Knowledge and experience of other managers involved in the SID process	**14.6**	**50.6**	**18.0**	**83.2**	**10.1**	**5.6**	**1.1**
Others (*please specify n* = 2)	**2.2**	**0**	**0**	**2.2**	**0**	**0**	**0**

21. **Did your views of the project change as a result of receiving more up-to-date (real-time) information about the following? (*n* = 91)**

	Yes	No
Change in the definition of the project (*n* = 89)	**42.7**	**57.3**
Technological issues (*n* = 90)	**42.2**	**57.8**
Logistical issues (*n* = 88)	**47.7**	**52.3**
The impact of financial projections (*n* = 89)	**68.5**	**31.5**
The need to act quickly to meet datelines (*n* = 89)	**50.6**	**49.4**
Other information (*please specify n* = 4)	**4.4**	**–**

22. **To what extent were the following aspects of the SID considered problematic?** (*please rank on a scale of 5 – to a great extent to 1 – hardly at all*)

(*n* = 91)

	To a great extent 5	4	3	OLS	2	Hardly at all 1	Not applicable
Specific objectives of the SID	**4.5**	**15.9**	**22.7**	**43.1**	**26.1**	**27.3**	**3.5**
Overall strategic objectives of the organisation	**8.0**	**22.7**	**15.9**	**46.6**	**23.9**	**26.1**	**3.4**
Procedures for evaluating the SID	**1.1**	**14.4**	**34.4**	**49.9**	**28.9**	**18.9**	**2.3**
Personal agendas	**4.6**	**20.7**	**16.1**	**41.4**	**20.7**	**33.3**	**4.6**
The pace at which matters should proceed	**7.9**	**39.3**	**31.5**	**78.7**	**9.0**	**7.9**	**4.4**
Issues of professional ethics and responsibility	**2.2**	**6.7**	**6.7**	**15.6**	**17.8**	**51.0**	**15.6**
The track record of the proposer of the SID	**3.3**	**11.1**	**13.3**	**27.7**	**20.1**	**37.8**	**14.4**
Others (*please specify n = 4*)	**2.1**	**2.2**	**0**	**4.4**	**0**	**0**	**0**

23. **To what extent did you have access to the following information for your specific project?** (*please rank on a scale of 5 – to a great extent to 1 – hardly at all, the extent to which the information was available*) **(*n* = 91)**

	To a great extent					Hardly at all	Not applicable
	5	**4**	**3**	**OLS**	**2**	**1**	
Market research (e.g. market size, share, growth, competitors' action and product price changes)	**20.9**	**34.1**	**20.9**	**75.9**	**9.9**	**5.5**	**8.7**
Information on customers/users	**18.7**	**44.0**	**23.1**	**85.8**	**6.6**	**0**	**7.6**
Supply chain information	**22.0**	**30.8**	**25.2**	**78.0**	**5.5**	**5.5**	**11.0**
Suppliers' views	**4.4**	**22.2**	**24.4**	**51.0**	**20.0**	**14.5**	**14.5**
Views of employees at operational level	**12.1**	**26.4**	**26.4**	**64.9**	**17.6**	**13.2**	**4.3**
Information on shareholders' views	**4.4**	**17.6**	**9.9**	**31.9**	**17.6**	**22.0**	**28.5**
Other stakeholders information, e.g. government	**6.6**	**15.4**	**15.4**	**37.4**	**8.8**	**27.5**	**26.3**
Financial projections	**50.5**	**31.9**	**12.1**	**94.5**	**2.2**	**0**	**3.3**
Business risk factors	**35.2**	**41.8**	**17.6**	**94.6**	**4.4**	**0**	**1.0**
Others (*please specify n = 3*)	**2.2**	**1.1**	**0**	**3.3**	**0**	**0**	**0**

24. Were any of the following used during the SID process? (*please indicate whether or not the process is applicable in your company and whether or not you were involved in the process*) (*n* = 91)

	Does it apply in your company?	Were you involved?
Informal (ad hoc rather than routine, planned within shorter notice) meetings	87.9	78.0
Corridor (unscheduled) meetings and internal lobbying	69.2	51.6
Political lobbying with external agencies, e.g. government department and trade associations	33.0	13.2
Using informal opportunities (e.g. at social functions) to influence decision-making	41.8	16.5
Other informal process(es): *please specify* *(n = 1)*	1.1	1.1

25. For the specific project, to what extent did each of the following alter your opinion on the SID? (*please rank on a scale of 5 – to a great extent to 1 – hardly at all*) (*n* = 91)

	To a great extent					Hardly at all	Not applicable
	5	4	3	OLS	2	1	
Discussion during formal meetings	15.4	38.5	31.9	85.8	7.6	6.6	0
Informal discussions and interaction with managers involved in the SID	14.3	39.6	27.5	81.4	12.1	5.4	1.1
Discussions and interaction with other managers not involved in the SID	2.2	7.7	27.5	37.4	26.4	30.7	5.5

(*Continued*)

	To a great extent					Hardly at all	Not applicable
Views of the company's top management[†]	**18.9**	**38.9**	**24.4**	**82.2**	**11.1**	**3.4**	**3.3**
Others (*please specify n = 2*)	**1.1**	**1.1**	**0**	**2.2**	**0**	**0**	**0**

[†]*For this research study, we have defined 'top management' to include head office management, senior management or group management. As the use of the term may differ from company to company, please keep this in mind when completing this questionnaire.*

26. **To what extent did the following occur during the SID?** (*please rank on a scale of 5 – to a great extent to 1 – hardly at all*) **(*n* = 91)**

	To a great extent					Hardly at all	Not applicable
	5	**4**	**3**	**OLS**	**2**	**1**	
People formed temporary alliances or subgroups expressly for the purpose of this SID	**12.2**	**22.2**	**22.2**	**56.6**	**13.3**	**23.3**	**6.8**
Disagreement was evident during the SID process	**4.4**	**23.3**	**28.9**	**56.6**	**23.3**	**16.8**	**3.3**
The proposer's track record with SIDs influenced the SID	**7.8**	**20.0**	**22.2**	**50.0**	**21.1**	**18.9**	**10.0**

(*Continued*)

	To a great extent					Hardly at all	Not applicable
Agreement was reached after considerable compromise	**1.1**	**10.0**	**15.6**	**26.7**	**36.7**	**27.8**	**8.8**
other examples of group behaviour (*please specify n = 11*)	5.5	2.2	3.3	11.0	0	1.1	–

27. **To what extent was each of the following important in gaining a consensus on the SID?** (*please rank on a scale of 5 – to a great extent to 1 – hardly at all*) **(*n* = 91)**

	To a great extent					Hardly at all	Not applicable
	5	**4**	**3**	**OLS**	**2**	**1**	
Managers who are socially compatible	**4.5**	**9.1**	**23.9**	**37.5**	**25.0**	**31.8**	**5.7**
Like-minded managers with similar experience in the industry	**10.3**	**36.8**	**31.0**	**78.1**	**12.6**	**5.8**	**3.5**
Managers with very different experiences	**7.9**	**25.8**	**40.4**	**74.1**	**16.9**	**4.5**	**4.5**
Managers with very different skills	**11.4**	**39.8**	**27.3**	**78.5**	**12.5**	**3.4**	**5.6**

(*Continued*)

	To a great extent					Hardly at all	Not applicable
Managers who speak their minds forthrightly	**23.6**	**32.6**	**31.5**	**87.7**	**5.5**	**3.4**	**3.4**
Managers who respect superiors' opinions	**5.6**	**18.0**	**28.1**	**51.7**	**18.0**	**22.5**	**7.8**
Managers trained in negotiating skills	**6.7**	**22.5**	**34.8**	**64.0**	**14.6**	**14.6**	**6.8**
Others (*please specify n* = 5)	**4.4**	**1.1**	**0**	**5.5**	**0**	**0**	**0**

28. **To what extent was each of the following used to assess the risk(s) associated with the SID(s)?** (*please rank on a scale of 5 – to a great extent to 1 – hardly at all*) **(*n* = 91)**

	To a great extent					Hardly at all	Not applicable
	5	**4**	**3**	**OLS**	**2**	**1**	
Evaluation of expected outcomes (based on probability or likelihood of alternative outcomes)	**34.4**	**31.1**	**11.1**	**76.6**	**10.0**	**8.9**	**4.5**
Comparison with risk profile of past projects	**14.6**	**27.0**	**19.1**	**60.7**	**19.1**	**13.5**	**6.7**

(*Continued*)

	To a great extent					Hardly at all	Not applicable
Intuition	**3.4**	**30.7**	**20.5**	**54.6**	**26.1**	**14.8**	**4.5**
Others (*please specify n = 16*)	**7.7**	**4.4**	**1.1**	**13.2**	**1.1**	**0**	**3.3**

29. To what extent does your company require each of the following during SID-making process? (*please rank on a scale of 5 – to a great extent to 1 – hardly at all*) **(*n* = 91)**

	To a great extent					Hardly at all	Not applicable
	5	**4**	**3**	**OLS**	**2**	**1**	
A set of standard procedures (e.g. following a procedures manual or standard instructions) to be employed when assessing SIDs	**25.6**	**30.0**	**18.9**	**74.5**	**10.0**	**7.8**	**7.7**
Assumptions underlying your decision to be stated	**52.2**	**30.0**	**14.4**	**96.6**	**2.2**	**1.2**	**0**
Top management's approval	**76.7**	**21.1**	**1.1**	**98.9**	**1.1**	**0**	**0**
Dissenting opinions to be reported	**9.0**	**16.9**	**25.8**	**51.7**	**23.6**	**19.1**	**5.6**

(*Continued*)

	To a great extent					Hardly at all	Not applicable
An individual manager to champion and be responsible for the SID	**44.4**	**25.6**	**21.1**	**91.1**	**3.3**	**2.2**	**3.4**
Others (*please specify n = 5*)	**3.3**	**1.1**	**0**	**4.4**	**0**	**1.1**	**0**

30. Which of the following Decision Support Software (DSS) did you use for appraising the SID (*n* = 91)

☐ Spreadsheet Model	**90.1**
☐ Specific Decision Support Package	**4.4**
☐ Decision Trees	**17.6**
☐ Critical Path Analysis	**50.5**
☐ Others (*please specify*)	**6.6**
☐ No DSS was used	**5.5**

Section D – Concluding section

31. To what extent is the SID-making process for the specific project you had in mind typical in your organisation in terms of the normal procedures used in your organisation? (*n* = 91)

To a great extent					Hardly at all
5	**4**	**3**	**OLS**	**2**	**1**
29.7	**50.5**	**13.3**	**93.5**	**4.4**	**1.1**

32. What suggestions would you offer to improve the SID-making process in your organisation? (*n* = 38)

Appendix 3: Further Statistical Tables: For Questions Using Likert Scales

Question 18 – The extent to which the following were used during the SID

	N	Minimum	Maximum	Mean	Standard deviation
Gut feeling or hunches or flashes of ideas	91	0	5	2.44	1.213
Mental pictures of the SID	90	0	5	2.96	1.323
Brainstorming	90	0	5	3.06	1.360
Industry's rule of thumb	90	0	5	2.60	1.347
Valid *N* (listwise)	89				

Question 19 – The level of importance of the following during the SID

	N	Minimum	Maximum	Mean	Standard deviation
Comparing and contrasting new with previous	91	0	5	3.49	1.345

(Continued)

	N	Minimum	Maximum	Mean	Standard deviation
Use of stereotypes to classify projects	87	0	5	1.95	1.284
Use of base value from previous project(s) and tolerance ranges	90	0	5	2.90	1.281
Use of industry benchmark	87	0	5	2.85	1.491
Use of other benchmarks	36	0	5	3.03	1.828
Valid *N* (listwise)	34				

Question 20 – The level of importance of aspects of personal knowledge and experience in influencing the SID

	N	Minimum	Maximum	Mean	Standard deviation
Technical experience	90	0	5	3.34	1.291
Managerial experience	90	0	5	3.74	1.176
Knowledge of competitors	89	0	5	2.90	1.438
Own professional background	90	0	5	3.98	0.861
Knowledge of inner workings or processes	90	0	5	4.12	0.872
Knowledge of strategy formulation	90	0	5	3.81	0.959
Knowledge and experience of other managers	89	0	5	3.55	1.108
Others	2	5	5	5.00	0.000
Valid *N* (listwise)	2				

Question 22 – The extent to which the following were problematic during the SID

	N	Minimum	Maximum	Mean	Standard deviation
Specific objectives of the SID	88	0	5	2.34	1.258
Overall strategic objectives of the organisation	88	0	5	2.52	1.389
Procedures for evaluating the SID	90	0	5	2.43	1.061
Personal agendas	87	0	5	2.29	1.363
The pace at which matters should proceed	89	0	5	3.17	1.227
Issues of professional ethics and responsibility	90	0	5	1.44	1.172
The track record of the proposer of the SID	90	0	5	1.79	1.345
Others	4	4	5	4.50	0.577
Valid *N* (listwise)	4				

Question 23 – The extent to which the following information were accessible during the SID

	N	Minimum	Maximum	Mean	Standard deviation
Market research	91	0	5	3.29	1.493
Information on customers or users	91	0	5	3.52	1.303
Supply chain information	91	0	5	3.25	1.553
Suppliers' views	90	0	5	2.39	1.459

(Continued)

	N	Minimum	Maximum	Mean	Standard deviation
Views of employees at operational level	91	0	5	2.93	1.365
Information on shareholders' views	91	0	5	1.79	1.595
Other stakeholders (e.g. government) information	91	0	5	1.86	1.644
Financial projections	91	0	5	4.21	1.101
Business risks factors	91	0	5	4.04	0.942
Others	3	4	5	4.67	0.577
Valid *N* (listwise)	3				

Question 25 – The extent to which the following altered opinions during the SID

	N	Minimum	Maximum	Mean	Standard deviation
Discussion during formal meetings	91	1	5	3.48	1.058
Informal discussions and interactions	91	0	5	3.42	1.116
Discussions and interactions with managers not involved	91	0	5	2.08	1.147
Views of companies top management	90	0	5	3.49	1.211
Others	2	4	5	4.50	0.707
Valid *N* (listwise)	2				

Question 26 – The extent to which the following occurred during the SID

	N	Minimum	Maximum	Mean	Standard deviation
Temporary alliances or subgroups formed	90	0	5	2.67	1.514

(Continued)

	N	Minimum	Maximum	Mean	Standard deviation
Disagreement evident	90	0	5	2.66	1.229
Proposer's track record influenced the SID	90	0	5	2.47	1.455
Agreement reached after considerable compromise	90	0	5	1.93	1.140
Other examples of group behaviour	11	1	5	3.91	1.300
Valid *N* (listwise)	11				

Question 27 – The level of importance of the following in gaining consensus during the SID

	N	Minimum	Maximum	Mean	Standard deviation
Managers who are socially compatible	88	0	5	2.13	1.249
Like-minded managers (similar experience)	87	0	5	3.23	1.188
Managers with very different experiences	89	0	5	3.02	1.158
Managers with very different skills	88	0	5	3.26	1.255
Managers who speak their minds forthrightly	89	0	5	3.57	1.205
Managers who respect superiors' opinions	89	0	5	2.43	1.373
Managers trained in negotiating skills	89	0	5	2.72	1.331
Others	5	4	5	4.80	0.447
Valid *N* (listwise)	4				

Question 28 – The extent to which the following were used to assess risks during the SID

	N	Minimum	Maximum	Mean	Standard deviation
Evaluation of expected outcomes (probability)	90	0	5	3.59	1.491
Comparison with risk profile of past projects	89	0	5	2.90	1.485
Intuition	88	0	5	2.68	1.273
Others	16	0	5	3.50	1.932
Valid *N* (listwise)	14				

Question 29 – The extent to which the following were required during the SID

	N	Minimum	Maximum	Mean	Standard deviation
Set of standard procedures	90	0	5	3.32	1.535
Assumptions underlying the decision stated	90	1	5	4.30	0.880
Top management's approval	90	2	5	4.73	0.536
Dissenting opinions to be reported	89	0	5	2.56	1.365
Individual manager to champion and be responsible	90	0	5	3.97	1.240
Others	5	1	5	4.00	1.732
Valid *N* (listwise)	4				

Question 31 – The extent to which the SID-making process is typical to the organisation

	N	Minimum	Maximum	Mean	Standard deviation
SID-making process typical in company	90	1	5	4.04	0.847
Valid *N* (listwise)	90				

Appendix 4: Case Analysis

This appendix illustrates the application of the descriptive model formulated from the survey results (Figure 5.1) for six case companies. Four of the six companies (I to IV) were large multinational corporations (MNCs), three of which had provided two or more responses to the CIMA survey and at least one respondent agreed to a follow-up interview. The fourth company was approached by the research team after the survey and several managers then answered the same survey questions. The other two (cases V and VI) were medium-sized enterprises (MSEs), where at least one manager agreed to be interviewed and answer the same set of questions as in the survey. Data for the case analysis is therefore taken from the survey questions as well as from the follow-up interviews and other company information (including SID procedure manuals in two cases). In total the data is drawn from 15 survey responses and nine interviews in the six case companies.

This appendix follows the structure from Figure 5.1, considering the organisational context for SID-making, managerial judgement and the SID process before drawing conclusions on the applicability of the descriptive model and its use in future SID research.

Organisational context

Table A4.1 shows the industry sector, size and strategic context of the organisation, the types of SID and the nature of the SID process in terms of the level of formality, the number of stages and the participation of multiple managers. Cases I to IV are all very large companies, with turnover in excess of five billion pounds and more than 10,000 employees. Cases V and VI are both medium sized, with turnover of approximately five million pounds and more than 60 employees. All operate in a global marketplace and have significant operations and/or sales to customers overseas.

With the exception of case V (founded in the 1990s), all organisations had a long history which tends to influence the organisational culture (Handy, 1993, p. 192), but had experienced a merger or other significant restructuring in the 1990s. Cases II and IV were restructured most recently in 2006. All four, very large companies had a hierarchical structure, with a high level of formality.

Table A4.1 The organisational context of cases

Case	I	II	III	IV	V	VI
Industry	Steel and other metals	Utility	Beverages	Chemicals	Healthcare	Camera equipment
Size	Large group	Large UK division	Large group	Large group	Medium	Medium
Strategic context	In top three steel producers in EU	Leading player in UK energy market	Leading brewer in UK/EU	20% share of world industrial gas market	Contracts with NHS, expanding overseas	Top lens producer for film industry
Types of SID	Mergers and acquisitions	New market and site development	New product development	New market development	New market and site development	Advanced technology
SID process	Bureaucratic, rule-bound Well-documented process Formal SID teams			Simple and informal Not documented No formal SID teams		
SID stages	1. Company strategy 2. Ideas and opportunities 3. Preliminary assumptions 4. Internal board views 5. Detailed assumptions 6. Scenario planning and risk analysis	1. Investment definition 2. Assignment of roles and responsibilities 3. Ascertainment of approval body 4. Strategic evaluation 5. Economic evaluation 6. Risk analysis and sensitivities	1. Project opportunities 2. Project definition 3. Business case 4. Regional manager's views 5. Financial data 6. Evaluation and risk analysis 7. Executive committee's opinions	1. Development of opportunities 2. Generation of project data 3. Assumptions 4. Financial models 5. Investment paper 6. Investment paper's review 7. Project approval 8. Implementation	1. Project generation 2. Project data 3. Assumptions 4. Senior managers' views 5. Informal evaluation and risk analysis 6. Project promotion 7. Authorisation 8. Implementation	1. Generation of ideas and opportunities 2. Market information 3. Model building 4. Board criteria 5. Authorisation 6. Implementation

	7. Independent arbiter's technical views 8. Group board criteria 9. Measured outcomes	7. Scheme paper approval 8. Implementation 9. Post-investment review	8. Authorisation 9. Change management 10. Implementation and testing 11. Post-completion evaluation	9. Post-completion review	Note: not followed in every case	
Participation						
Business development	■	■	■	■	□	□
Finance managers	■	■	■	■	■	■
Directors/ CEO	■	■	■	■	■	■
Operations/ production	■	■	■	□	■	■
Project managers	■	□	■	□	□	□
Others	HR and technical managers	Engineering managers	R&D managers	ICT managers	IT manager	Chairman

With the exception of case III (a brand-led organisation with a history dominated by some well-known characters in the business, thus elements of autocracy), the large companies would all be considered heavily bureaucratic or rule-bound.

Smaller companies tend to have a dominant character holding the key power position, usually the majority shareholder, who may appear as a Zeus-type business leader (Handy, 1993, p. 183). Cases V and VI were no exception, though case VI also showed signs of a task culture, with high levels of innovation and considerable space for creativity.

Cases I and IV rely on industrial customers, so are affected by the economics of world manufacturing. Case II operates in an energy market regulated by governments, so is influenced by world politics, especially environmental aspirations. Case III is a brand leader in the alcoholic drinks market, so is influenced by social trends, e.g. a decline in beer drinking in the UK. Both cases V and VI are operating in niche or specialist markets, but case V is influenced by government health policy, whereas case VI is technology led. This influences the type of strategic investments being considered.

All companies identified at least six stages in their SID process, which were generally well aligned to the 10 stages distilled from earlier studies used to formulate the survey questions (Box 1.1). There are fewer stages (six and eight) in the MSEs as we might expect, and more steps in the larger MNCs (nine in cases I, II and IV and eleven in case III). The nature of those stages is similar, but in case I it is more top-down as appropriate for business acquisitions and in case III it includes change management.

SIDs in the large MNCs involved business development managers, not found in the MSEs. Finance managers and directors were involved in SID-making in all six cases, and operations or production managers were involved in all except case IV, though they did involve what they called business unit managers. Project managers were only identified as involved in the SID process in two organisations (I and III), which may mean the others do not manage the implementation stage of SIDs as 'projects' as defined in project management terms. The cases that involved project managers were acquisitions and new product developments, where change management is either implicit or explicit.

The other participants identified all had technical type roles in cases I to V. Only case VI identified the chairman as involved in SIDs, which is understandable in a smaller organisation, where the chairman also undertook a sales management role. The section 'Managerial judgement' explores the nature of managerial judgement applied in the six companies and the section 'SID process' explores the nature of managerial involvement at the different stages in the SID process.

Managerial judgement

Table A4.2 shows the types of heuristics or reference points used and the company requirements and processes for presentation of project proposals and reaching agreement. These are broadly categorised into those that may be seen as enabling

(E) managerial judgement, drawing on intuition and business knowledge, and those that may be seen as constraining (C) managerial judgement by imposing a prescribed format for decision-making information.

One might expect that decision-making in the MNCs would be more formalised and therefore constraining and that the MSEs would allow more freedom to individual managers to use their judgement and therefore enabling. However, the pattern of results does not follow this expectation exactly. Cases I, II, III and V appeared to be the most enabling in terms of the use of brainstorming (intuition), comparisons with past projects (anchoring and adjustment) and a range of other reference points. Cases IV and V1 produced a more mixed result.

The pattern was quite different when it came to the framing of proposals, where cases II to V more or less conformed to expectations. Case I appeared to be far more enabling than expected and case VI perhaps more constraining than expected, though they did use brainstorming in the board room. The contrast between the results for heuristics and framing may be seen as revealing a tension between the formality in the SID process imposed by top management and the preference shown by individual managers for using their intuition and 'gut feel' based on their business knowledge and experience. Having said that, the distance between top management control and managers participating in SID teams is not so great in the MSEs, so this distinction is harder to make in cases V and VI.

Case I really stands out from the others in this analysis, where both the heuristics and framing appear to enable managerial judgement far more than in the other MNCs. Informal and highly political processes appeared to be important in gaining consensus, although the managers rarely encountered temporary alliances. The socio-political process was described by the interviewee:

> *Because we want the project approval process to go on smoothly, we make sure that anybody that may have a contrary view is dealt with before it gets to the final decision-making process. Our managers tend to view things independently and if they don't like something then they will say it. Particularly when we are dealing with big financial decisions, then managers are always a bit edgy about whether it is the right thing to go ahead with. And we strive to avoid someone questioning some of the bases during the final decision stage. So the solution is to do all the behind-the-scene works because it is too dangerous not to, and a lot of problems get ironed out behind the scenes. As a result we end up with a far better proposal that looks far more likely to succeed, and go through the entire SID process without a problem (case I, manager 1).*

The consensus-seeking process involves wide consultation and a significant amount of interaction behind the scenes by the project champion to gauge and shape

Table A4.2 Managerial judgement (heuristics, framing and consensus) in case companies

Case	I	II	III	IV	V	VI
Industry	Steel and other metals	Utility	Beverages	Chemicals	Healthcare	Camera equipment
Heuristics						
Brainstorming	considerable (E)	considerable (E)	considerable (E)	Not used (C)	considerable (E)	Used (E)
Comparisons with past	considerable (E)	considerable (E)	considerable (E)	considerable (E)	Very influential (E)	Not used, due to the novelty of projects
Knowledge of:						
– industry/ competition	– most important	–	– quite important	– quite important	– quite important	– lack of information
– inner workings	– quite important	– most important	– most important	– most important	– quite important	– most important
– strategy formulation	– most important	– quite important	– most important	– quite important	– quite important	– most important
Experience of:						
– managerial	– most important	– quite important	– most important	– not important	– most important	– most important
– professional	– most important	– quite important	– most important	– most important	– most important	– quite important
– technical	– quite important	– quite important	– most important	– quite important	– most important	–
Other influences	External/ independence and cynicism (E)	Knowledge/ experience of other managers (E)	Views of top management (C)	Knowledge/ experience of other managers (E)		Intuition guided by gut feel (E)
	Wide consultation	Informal discussions	No informal discussions	Informal discussions	Limited SID information	Informal discussions

Framing	*Enabling* ■ Company emphasised the presentation of real-time information ■ Company required project data presented in a manner that shows its strategic fit ■ Managers used own models *Constraining* ■ Presentation of comprehensive evaluations quickened the SID process ■ Level of scrutiny	*Enabling* ■ Variety of acceptability indicators *Constraining* ■ Company provided managers with a standard template for presentation of project information ■ Lack of knowledge of strategy formulation and	*Constraining* ■ Detailed/ comprehensive presentation of data analyses evaluations and sensitivity and risk analysis required ■ Presentation of models analysing the data, financial impact of project, IT impact of project, stakeholder analysis and cultural assessment required ■ Use of spreadsheets, project management software and decision trees	*Constraining* ■ Formal and	*Enabling* ■ 'Off-the-cuff' presentation of information – this appeared to force managers to use more cognitive heuristics (mental pictures) *Constraining* ■ MD's views dominated	*Constraining* ■ Detailed comprehensive presentation of relevant financial and non-financial market information required ■ Presentation of business and cost models analysing the information required

(*Continued*)

Table A4.2 (*Continued*)

Case	I	II	III	IV	V	VI
Consensus Important factors in gaining consensus – managers:	*Mixed bag: Consensus managed by different managers in different ways*	*Consensus managed by different managers in similar ways*	*Consensus managed by different managers in similar ways:* 'singular focus, huge team work'	*Consensus managed by different managers in similar ways*	*Two conflicting views:* – *gaining consensus was not an issue (MD)* – *gaining consensus was an issue (others)*	*The company's philosophy of 'no shocks' encouraged open dialogue*
– who are socially compatible (C)	Not important	Most important	Quite important	Quite important	Most important	Quite important
– with similar experience (C)	....	....	....	....	....	Most important
– with very different skills (E)	Quite important	Most important	Most important	Most important	Not important	Most important
– who speak their minds forthrightly (E)	....	....	....	....	....	Most important
– who respect superiors' views (C)	Not important	Most important	Not important	Most important	Most important	Quite important
– trained in negotiating skills (E)	....	Most important	....	Not important	Not important	Most important

Personal agendas considered as problematic (E)	Managers frequently encountered personal agendas, some found them problematic	Managers frequently encountered personal agendas and found them most problematic	Managers frequently encountered personal agendas: most did not find them problematic, but dissenters were isolated	Managers frequently encountered personal agendas and found them slightly problematic	Managers frequently encountered personal agendas but did not find them problematic as only one view counted	Managers frequently encountered personal agendas and found them most problematic
Temporary alliances were formed (E)	Rarely	Frequently	Frequently	Never	Rarely	Frequently
Overall, consensus achieved by	Reaching agreement	Constrained agreement	Constrained agreement	Constrained agreement	Decree	Reaching agreement

the views of other managers, so enabling managerial judgement in the decision-making process.

Managers in cases II, III and VI encountered the formation of temporary alliances to a greater extent than the others, which might be expected more in larger bureaucratic firms, but not necessarily in the technology-driven MSE. They also found personal agendas more problematic than managers in the other organisations.

One interviewee in case II (manager 2) emphasised the importance of the views of the leadership team and the Audit Committee in gaining approval for projects. Another interviewee in the same organisation described the consensus-seeking process:

We do a lot of stakeholder management before we get to present the project proposal. So we might be in talking to our senior managers to extract a view from them whether there is going to be an issue regarding it or whether it is going to a sign on. To ensure easy progression through the company, we get a lot of managers to support the project (case II, manager 1).

In case III it was noted that dissenters would be isolated, which may explain why the personal agendas were not seen as problematic by three out of four managers. There was a strong sense of top management control coming through the data collected from this organisation. This may mean that some of the managerial judgement exercised through brainstorming and other creative processes was effectively stifled later in the process.

This formality is also evident in case IV, where the SID process is closely controlled by the Corporate Finance function, with three stages of decision-making at business unit, investment committee and group board levels. Interviewees made very little comment on consensus seeking other than following set procedures, which allows little scope for managerial judgement.

In contrast, managers in case V said they used their knowledge and experience a great deal in exercising managerial judgement, often with minimal information about the project. One manager commented:

The project is talked about in a very informal way and most of the opinions you put forward are often based on how you visualise the project, how you think it would work out. Again this would draw on your experience and professional background. The opinions would be based on prior similar experiences; and how you deal with people... (case V, manager 1).

However, as with case IV, managers in case V viewed consensus as a non-issue:

Because of the powers of the MD, disagreement is not very evident, because people don't want to be seen as disagreeing with the MD. You don't want to be that guy who is not on the side of the MD (case V, manager 1).

We don't really have a situation where you would discuss issues until you reach a compromise, because of the fact that you have this one individual who is always masterminding the whole project. There is no room for discussions ....there is only room for one thing, support. ..... To me it is just like a typical family business (case V, manager 2).

A third manager echoed the same sense of top management constraint:

You are allowed to say whatever you want to say but whether the reactions of the MD will encourage you to do that in the future is a different ball game altogether. I would personally say, from my experience, that the reactions and actions of the director do not encourage us. Of course no one is going to stop you from putting across your views, but whether the MD takes it on board or not tells you what to do in future. I would say that the actions and reactions of top management do not encourage meaningful discussions of the investments (case V, manager 3).

These comments all point to there being no place at all for managerial judgement other than by the MD in the decision-making in this organisation, which is in stark contrast to the survey responses to the heuristics and framing questions for this firm, which seemed quite enabling.

Whilst case VI shares some similar characteristics in terms of organisational context, it appears to have inherited more of a large firm culture, perhaps due to its history, with the formation of temporary alliances and problems with personal agendas. The reason given by the manager interviewed for not having too much problem with reaching consensus was that open dialogue was encouraged from the start, described as a 'no shocks philosophy'. While part of the process in case VI was similar to the other MSE, there was no impression of the MD or the chairman stifling the views of other managers as the MD in case V appeared to.

SID process

Table A4.3 shows the level of involvement of participating managers, decision support techniques, any variation in the agendas or purpose of internal meetings and the external parties consulted. Whilst the level of involvement varied within and between cases, there was strong evidence for the following agenda areas for internal meetings, which all attempted to:

- gather views (all except case VI)
- evaluate risks (all except case IV attached probabilities)
- construct models (all except cases IV and V)
- identify key/critical success factors (all except case VI)
- reach consensus, decide on the desirability of the project and conclude on is-

Table A4.3 SID process (level of involvement, meetings and externals consulted)

Case	I	II	III	IV	V	VI
Industry	Steel and other metals	Utility	Beverages	Chemicals	Healthcare	Camera equipment
Level of involvement of participating managers	Varied from minor to significant – roles the managers played depended on the manager concerned, and the formal SID team(s) the manager was in.	Varied from minor to significant – roles played depending on the managers concerned, value of project and required financial returns.	Varied – roles depended on manager and level in the organisational hierarchy.	Varied – roles depended on manager and level in the organisational hierarchy.	Varied – roles depended on the MD's choice, technical expertise and experience of the manager concerned.	All managers were encouraged to be heavily involved
Types of decision support used in addition to Excel spreadsheets	■ Decision trees ■ Critical path analysis	■ Critical path analysis	■ Decision trees ■ Critical path analysis ■ Tailor-made DSS ■ Stage-gate navigator process	■ Tailor-made DSS ■ Own Intranet-based system ■ Specialist support software for risk analysis		■ Critical path analysis

Variation in agenda or purpose of meetings	■ Set negotiating strategy		■ Established ground rules ■ Established project ownership ■ Eased implementation	■ Did not attach probabilities to alternative outcomes in evaluating risks	■ Did not handle any complexity by constructing models	■ Did not identify key success factors or ■ Gather views from various stakeholders
Externals consulted	■ Lawyers ■ Accountants ■ Investment bankers ■ Stock brokers ■ Competition analysts ■ Pension advisors ■ Target company ■ Finance organisations ■ Government departments	Use of external consultants determined at start of the process: ■ Technical managers from supplier organisation ■ Business development consultants ■ IT consultants Approval required where the cost exceeded £0.7 million	■ Suppliers ■ Legal counsels ■ Designers	Apparently none	■ Suppliers ■ Financing organisations ■ Government agencies	■ Project manager ■ Technical managers from suppliers' organisations ■ Financing organisations ■ Health and safety organisations

All six case organisations used Excel spreadsheets for decision support, though the responses to questions about framing (see Table A4.2) showed variation in whose models were used, the manager's own (enabling managerial judgement) or prescribed models. Three MNCs and one of the MSEs used project management software for critical path analysis. Cases I and III also used decision trees. Only case IV was using specialist risk analysis software.

The extent of external consultation varied, but not necessarily with size or any other of the organisational variables. It appears to vary more with the type of project being proposed, with case I (mergers and acquisitions focus) reporting the widest external consultation. Case IV did not appear to consult externally, which is perhaps understandable for market development type projects where marketing expertise is available internally.

The capacity of the organisation to manage consensus seems to be affected by the management style or organisational culture. Cases I, II, IV and VI seem to have greater capacity for seeking managers' views about proposals and managing a consensus-seeking process, where cases III and V do not manage by consensus but by a more autocratic process.

The 'no shocks' philosophy found in case VI captures the rationale for enabling managers to use their knowledge and experience in evaluating proposals, in that managerial judgement has more value before an important strategic decision is made than afterwards when strategic risks might not be avoidable. Top management hubris may account for a lack of open dialogue in cases III and V, making the SID process riskier than it need be.

The descriptive model drawn up from the survey data in Chapter 5 has been used to analyse these six cases and was helpful in comparing and contrasting the SID processes. The distinction between an enabling and a constraining process can be made in terms of how much influence managerial judgement has on the decision, though our cases show that few organisations are likely to be totally enabling or totally constraining. The surprise is that the role of managerial judgement is not as predictable from the size of the organisation as might be expected, though these six cases may not be sufficiently representative to draw a firm conclusion. However, the results suggest that other aspects such as organisational culture, leadership or management style and use of bespoke decision support systems are potentially more influential than size. The descriptive model offers sufficient explanation in these cases to conclude that it will be useful in guiding future research on SID-making. Managerial judgement appears to be more managed, enabled or constrained in individual companies and offers an intriguing insight to what constitutes an effective SID process.

Index

Lightning Source UK Ltd.
Milton Keynes UK
11 October 2009

144779UK00001B/75/P

9 781856 178235